RRY

HIEF

SPO...ES

...sie Parr, Joseph R. Garry
the reinterment of Nina
uly of 1962. Courtesy of

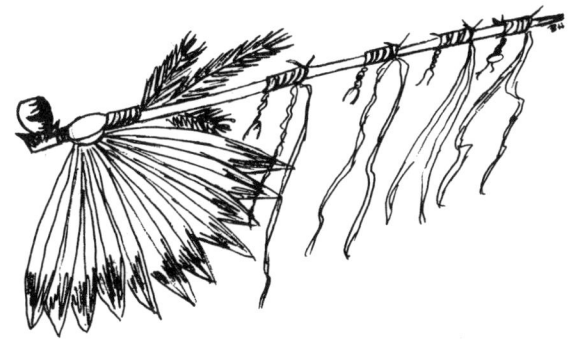

THE CASE OF SPOKANE GARRY

SPOKANE GARRY
As he appeared in his old age. Photograph by
Loryea, 1889.

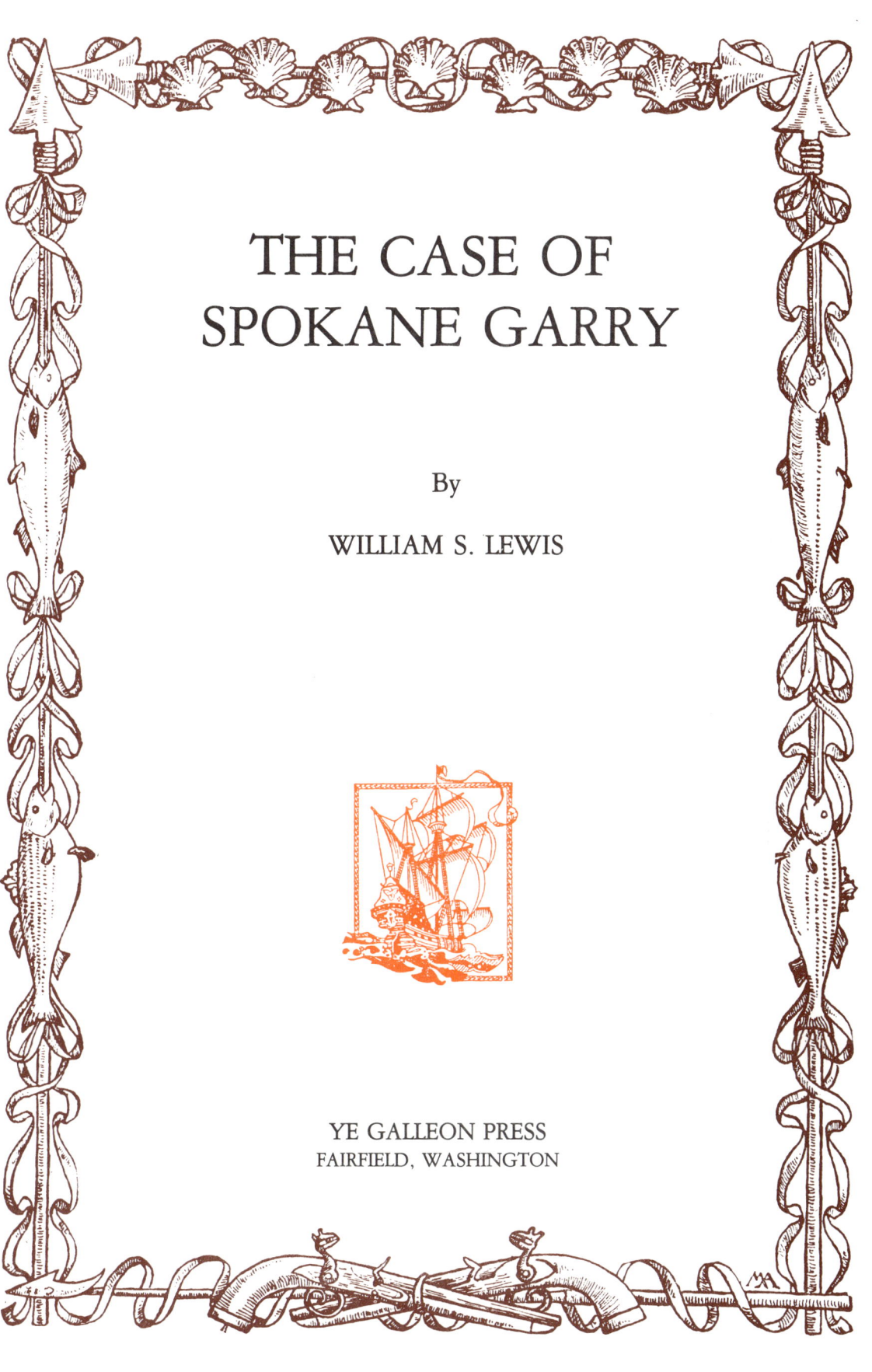

THE CASE OF SPOKANE GARRY

By

WILLIAM S. LEWIS

YE GALLEON PRESS
FAIRFIELD, WASHINGTON

Library of Congress Cataloging in Publication Data

Lewis, William S. (William Stanley), 1876-1941.
The case of Spokane Garry.

Reprint.
Bibliography: p.
Includes index.
1. Spokane Garry, 1811?-1892. 2. Spokan Indians—Biography.
3. Indians of North America—Washington (State)—Biography. 4. Spokan
Indians—Land tenure. 5. Indians of North America—Washington
(State)—Land tenure. I. Title.
E99.S68G313   1987   979.7'00497   87-10556
ISBN 0-87770-405-8

TABLE OF CONTENTS

PART I

THE FACTS IN THE CASE

CHAPTER I

CHAPTER II

CHAPTER III

CHAPTER IV

CHAPTER V

CHAPTER VI

PART II
THE CASE AGAINST GARRY

PART III

CONCLUSION

APPENDIX

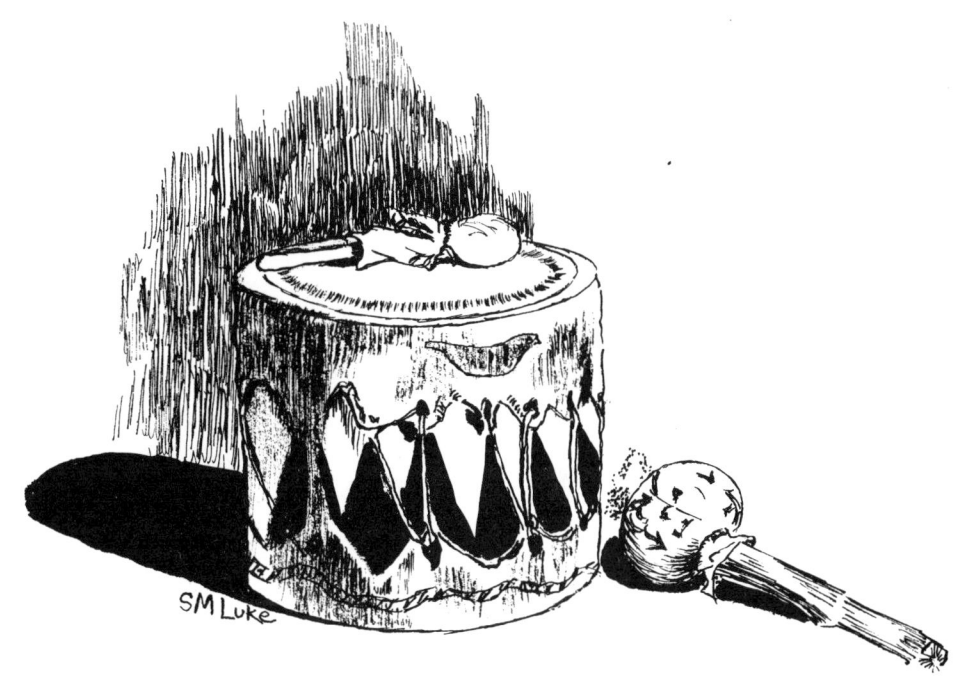

LIST OF ILLUSTRATIONS

PREFACE

A resident of the Spokane country for the past thirty-two years, I have during that time frequently heard Spokane Garry, late head chief of the Spokane Indians, referred to by "old timers" as an Indian who had fought the whites and was "Kul-tus," and for whom they entertained no respect.

An interest in the early history of the northwest having led me to read a number of diaries, letters, reports and accounts of occurrences in the "old Oregon" country during the early and middle part of the last century, I remarked that Spokane Garry had, in those early days, occupied a position of some slight importance, and had, to some degree, at least, commended himself to those with whom he was then associated.

The purpose and aim of this article is:—

To present a complete and accurate statement of the principal facts relative to the life and achievements of Spokane Garry, Head Chief of the Middle and Upper Spokane Indians: To fully discuss several charges made against Spokane Garry by later settlers and to apply the facts thereto: and to determine, as nearly as possible, what position Chief Garry's life record entitled him to hold in the history of the Northwest.

Some care has been taken to make no statement of fact except on reliable authority, and so far as possible, the authority for each statement is given in a footnote. In the preparation of this article the writer acknowledges the courtesy of J.M. Hitt, State Librarian, in furnishing him some authorities not available in local libraries, and the assistance of Hildegard J. Lewis in the preparation of the article.

William S. Lewis

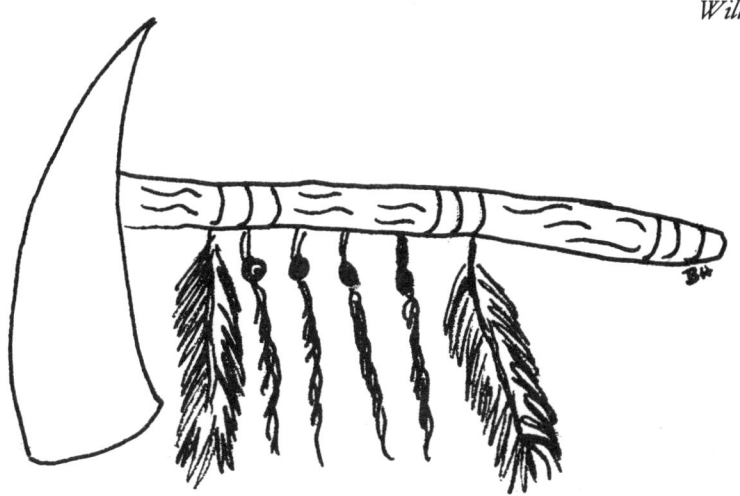

9

ACKNOWLEDGEMENTS

When the original edition of *The Case of Spokane Garry* was published in 1917 by the Spokane Historical Society there was a small membership in the group. No doubt because of this fact, there were few copies printed of that first edition. We feel that more readers should know about Spokane Garry and his place in Northwest History; therefore, this book, enlarged to add recently located sources, should find more readers eager to learn about this unusual man.

In researching a book of this kind, a writer owes a great debt of gratitude to many people.

Posthumous thanks to my good friend Richard T. Lewis, who photographed the Garry bibles as well as the photos of the reinterment of Nina Garry, the wife of Chief Spokane Garry. Dick told me I could use them as I wished and there is no better place for them to be shown than as illustrations for this book.

Thanks also to the late Josie Parr and Christine Ellenwood for the opportunity to photograph the Garry bibles. Their faith in Dick and I was commendable for they loaned those valuable family treasures to us so we could photograph them.

The Eastern Washington State Historical Society allowed Dick and I to use the Spokane Garry pipe and hand written booklet which appears in the illustrations in this volume along with the bibles.

Doug Olson of the above institution rendered unstinting aid in locating data.

Nancy Campau, Northwest Room Librarian at the Spokane Public Library also gave aid.

Especial thanks to my long suffering wife, La Verle, who has had to live through all of my writing phases. Love you.

JEROME PELTIER

INTRODUCTION

t is my intention to write an introduction to *The Case of Spokane Garry* that will add another dimension to that work. I am doing this because many accounts in which he is mentioned in a greater or lesser degree have appeared in print since 1917 when this classic of his life first appeared.

I want to share some family stories with you because I was fortunate indeed to have been able to interview Ignace Hayden Garry and his two half-sisters, Mrs. Christine Ellenwood and Josie Parr, great-grandchildren of Spokane Garry. Ignace gave me some eye-witness accounts of the old gentleman's life, because he lived with him in his latter years.

Christine Ellenwood, Josie Parr and Joseph Garry, the son of Ignace also remembered stories that were told in family gatherings, about Spokane Garry. They gladly shared these stories with me.

The life story of Spokane Garry in many ways reads very much like that of many Indian chiefs who went through periods of success and tribal approval prior to the advent of Caucasians into their area. After that happened there was a steady decline in fortune, to ultimate failure. Garry was to endure, with variations, the same experiences as other tribal leaders. Most accounts run pretty well in the same vein because as settlers pressed ever westward, natives were forced to move ahead of them or fight. The only other alternative to the above was to force their neighbors ahead of them in order to avoid bloody confrontations. Sometimes this pressure on their neighbors caused internecine warfare.

Garry was to experience white man's pleasures and cultures, and some of his vices. He was also to experience white man's encroachment that was finally to deprive him of his ancestral lands and eventually his very home, because he could not bring himself to change with the times.

The life of Spokane Garry was filled with elements that make great drama and because of this, the story of his experiences are well worth recording or, as in this case, the re-publishing of an old classic account of his life.

Spokane Garry was the son of Illum Spokanee, or with slight variations, a name much like it. His great-grandson Ignace Garry told me during an interview October 12, 1961, that Garry's father was known as Illum Eekum Spokanee. He did not elaborate on the middle part of the name but he did emphasize it. He did however, insist that the tribe should be called Spokanee. [I am inclined to agree with Ignace in both cases.]

In another interview, March 16, 1962, at the home of Christine Ellenwood and her sister Josie Parr, I questioned his statement. When I asked if there was "Eekum" between the two names, they both retorted that they hadn't heard it pronounced Illum Eekum Spokanee, and Mrs. Josie Parr volunteered that the shorter version meant "Chief of the Sun."

Mrs. Ellenwood said, "Illum Spokanee was the father of Spokane Garry. He didn't know who his mother was. She must have died when he was young."

The fact that the young man did not have a mother who would object to his being sent among strangers to the Red River Colony to be educated in the white man's language and religion made it easier for his father to decide that he could go with Governor George Simpson.

The governor was on a tour of the Northern Department of the Hudson's Bay Company, a large district under his supervision. His object during this visit to Spokane House, which lay at the junction of the Spokane and Little Spokane Rivers, was to decide whether he should close the facility which was being operated at great cost to the company, and transfer its operations to a location on the Columbia River, the then major arterial of travel into the interior of the Northwest. As a result of his evaluation, he ordered its closure and Fort Colville was built in 1826 near Kettle Falls to take its place.

The known facts of Spokane Garry's life began, as it was

documented at the forks of the Spokane River, when Simpson wrote under date of April 8, 1825: "Had a long interview with Eight Chiefs belonging to the Flat Head Coutanais Spokan and other tribes who assembled here for the purpose of seeing me; they appeared to be much pleased with all that was told them and promise well. Made them a present of a little ammunition and Tobacco. The Spokan and Flat Head Chiefs put a Son each under my care to be Educated at the Missionary Society School Red River and all the Chiefs joined in a most earnest request that a Missionary or religious instructor should be placed among them!"[1]

Four days later on April 12th, shortly after leaving Spokane House, Simpson added: . . ."Baptised the Indian Boys, they are the Sons of the principal Spokan and Coutonais War Chiefs, Men of great Weight and consequence in this part of the Country; they are named Coutonais Pelly and Spokan Garry."[2]

Alexander Ross, who was on his way to assume his new position as the superior officer at the Red River operations of the Company, wrote more fully about the two boys in his classic set of books *The Fur Hunters of the Far West* Vol. 11, pps. 157, 158. A complete quote of his remarks may be found in the main text of this book on pps. 12 and 13.

After five years at the school, Spokane Garry returned home filled with knowledge and enthusiasm. While the feeling lasted he convinced his people to build a school close to Spokane House and later still another near a spring close to Euclid and Maple Streets in present Spokane, Washington. Drumheller Spring, which lay below Spring Hill as pioneers called it, was a resting place for men and animals before they ascended the incline. It was also a camping site for the Spokane Indians. [It is well described by William S. Lewis on page 46 of the principal text.]

Visits by famous people, like W.H. Gray and Douglas, added their bit to our knowledge of Garry's life.

Spokane Garry attempted to obtain employment with the Hudson's Bay Co. He must have contacted Simon McGillivry[3] in order to do so because John McLoughlin answered his request by mail. The letter reads as follows:

Fort Vancouver
17th Augt 1832

Simon McGillivry Esq.
(Ft. Colvile)

Dear Sir:

    I have yours of the 15th July now before me and in reply if Spokane Garry is to be employed and in what capacity I have only to observe that your compliment unless something has occured out of the usual Routine is complete and besides I do not see in what capacity you can require his services or that he can be useful to you.—as to a person to take charge of the Kutanis post you may depend you will have one in due time, however as will have to address you on arrival of the Vessel from Nass I will then write more fully, will you send the Iron Corn Mill (if you don't require it) by the Express?

I am
Dear Sir
Yours truly

          signed   John McLoughlin.[4]

It appears from the above that Spokane Garry did not get the job he wanted.

Spokane Garry began to make contributions to the knowledge of his people not long after his return from the Red River Colony.

Summing some of them up, we find that he was the first teacher in the Pacific Northwest. His students were taught writing, English and religious subjects. It was claimed he brought religion into the area. This is quite a broad statement to make because there is reasonable proof that Catholic Iroquois Indians who came from the East were very religious and spread the gospel wherever they roamed. French fur traders, who were traditionally Catholic, did the same. These people professed their faith and thus influenced people they met. Jedediah Smith, a man who carried his bible with him wherever he went, must have shared his beliefs with others also.

Secondly Garry taught his people the science of agriculture. As evidenced by the amount of foodstuffs that were stored away and which were destroyed by Col. George Wright and his soldiers during the Indian campaign of 1858. The destruction of this food caused great anguish and hunger among the natives the following winter.[5]

Garry very likely taught his people the wisdom of raising their own cattle because Indian legend tells us that when Wright and his men destroyed grains and other foodstuffs, that they also killed the cattle that ranged in Spokane Valley. What sickened the natives was the fact that only the hind quarters of the animals were used and the remainder was left to rot.

Garry contributed toward what became known as *Etshiit*, the first book printed in the Spokane (Salish) language. Elkanah Walker[6] took credit for its publication. It was printed on the Lapwai press in 1842, but Garry's many visits to Tschimakain[7] between January 1841 and June 1842 must have borne some fruit as a result of the linguistic conferences between the two men.

Although he was considered a "profligate wretch," Garry was still asked to aid in the study of the Spokane language.[8] On Sunday, February 13, 1842 Walker wrote, "Made all my worships short and did not talk long, have been mostly on the Lord's prayer, and I have had it translated of late by Garry."[9]

During the period between May and June 1843 Garry was at Tschimakain (the Walker-Eells mission) and aided Walker, somewhat reluctantly, with the complilation of the Spokane language.[10]

On Tuesday, June 12, 1843 Walker wrote that Mr. (Cushing) Eells had a long conversation with him (Garry) and found out that it was the people who drove him off, not being able to withstand their ridicule.[11]

The statement made above explains why Garry lost interest in teaching his people.

To continue with Garry's contribution to the agricultural picture of this area, we must refer to William H. Gray, a secular member of the American Board of Commissioners for Foreign Missions, who in an April 1st, 1837 visit to the Spokane area wrote: —"This afternoon, we crossed over the [Spokane] River to see the Natives at this place, and the ground they cultivate, also a young Native that has been at school at Red River by the name of Garry. He has a considerable quantity of potatoes which, he said, Br. Spalding[12] may have what he wants of for seed."[13]

William H. Gray during another visit, wrote that the Spokane Indians were attentive to meetings of a religious character. He also wrote in his informative diary:—"They have a native school, taught by one of their own young men, who has received a limited education at Red River, by the name of Garry."

"They have also a house, devoted for Religious meetings sufficiently large to contain all the persons in the Village. Their worship is similar to that of the Nez Perces. Garry has a bible from which he attempts to teach the Natives. Having received his knowledge away from his tribe, he has in several instances imposed on their credulity by his superior knowledge."[14]

I asked Ignace Garry if he knew how Garry's school was constructed during an interview I had with him October 12, 1961 and he said "Nelly told Mrs. Ellenwood that they built some of their houses of tules. About like scatter rugs. These were stretched over a framework of small bent saplings. The ends of these dwellings were of tules too."

"During the same interview Ignace volunteered, we had some of his prints but someone took it. I had them but I might have thrown them away. I can't find them anyway. He had a church on the Spokane River. Some Coeur d'Alenes came to hear him. One Coeur d'Alene had a white deer skin and when Garry talked he wrote what he said down in some kind of shorthand. When the Coeur d'Alenes went back to Fort Coeur d'Alene one of them started telling the others what Garry had said. The man with the deer skin said 'you are wrong, and read from his deer skin what Garry had said.''

Garry's agricultural experiment must have paid excellent dividends because he felt that he had to have a mill to take care of wheat he and his people had grown.

What was later to be called the Oppenheimer, which was eventually built in the Colville Valley, was erected originally on the Little Spokane River for Spokane Garry. It was moved because of problems with Garry. (Indian accounts are the source for this story.)

W.P. Winans in a manuscript entitled *Stevens County, It's Creation, Addition, Subtraction and Division* gives the complete story from the white man's point of view.[15]

Garry must have raised a great deal of wheat in order to plan for the use of a grist mill.

During 1841 Governor Simpson made his third visit to the Spokane country and found a disillusioned Spokane Garry. The governor's comments show us just how much his friend had changed during the past decade.

Simpson was enroute to Fort Colville and was on the Pend Oreille River not too far away from Albeni Falls, when he saw the following things:—

> In one tent a sight presented itself, which was equally novel and unnatural. Surrounded by a crowd of spectators, a party of fellows were playing at cards obtained in the Snake country from some American trappers; and a more melancholy exemplification of the influence of civilization on barbarism could hardly be imagined than the apparently scientific eagerness with which these naked and hungry savages thumbed and turned the black and greasy pasteboard. Though the man who sold the cards might have taught the use of them, yet I could not help tracing the wretched exhibition to a more remote source—a source with which I was myself, in some measure connected. In this same hell of the wilderness, I found Spokan Garry, one of the lads already mentioned as having been sent to Red River for their education and there was little reason to doubt that, with his superior knowledge, he was the master spirit, if not the prime mover, of the scene. On his return to his countrymen, he had, for a time endeavored to teach them to read and write; but he had gradually abandoned the attempt,

17

assigning as his reason or his pretext that the others "Jawed him so much about it." He forthwith relapsed into his original barbarism, taking to himself as many wives as he could get; and then, becoming a gambler, he lost both all that he had of his own and all that he could beg or borrow from others. He was evidently ashamed of his proceedings, for he would not come out of the tent to shake hands even with an old friend.[16]

Governor Simpson was incorrect when he wrote that Garry had as many wives as he could get. He had two.

Mrs. Christine Ellenwood, during an interview on Thursday, July 10, 1958 told me about her great-grandmother, Garry's second wife:—"Nina was a teenager at the time she married Spokane Garry. She was a Umatilla."

Later on during the same interview, Mrs. Ellenwood added some interesting family history. "One of his first teachers was a woman named Nina and another was Nelly. He named his wife and daughter after these two teachers." She added, "Our people tried to learn English but eventually gave up while Garry taught them. This was at old Garry Spring in Spokane.[17] Tom Paul was a student of Garry's school."

Garry had married an older girl named Lucy prior to his marriage to Nina. Lucy lived near Spokane House and was the mother of another family by Garry.

On September 1, 1841, Spokane Garry was seen by Reverend H.H. Spalding when he and Mrs. Spalding visited the Spokane country. Spalding asked Garry to visit him and noted that "Garry comes by my request. Poor creature how miserable he looks I speak of the present and future prospects and urge him to abandon his gambling but he seems lost."—[18]

Garry evidently had a change of heart later on in his life because he wrote to Spalding March 27, 1873 and asked him "to baptize his people and marry them according to the laws."[19]

At the end of the year 1845, Mary Walker, the wife of Elkanah made a very revealing statement about their lack of success as missionaries when she wrote:—

"Wed. 31. The close of another year. A year of health and prosperity, but as [a] Mission we seem to have affected little. Oh! that it would please God and open the eyes of this people."[20]

Perhaps some of the apathy shown by Garry rubbed off on his tribesmen with the results mentioned above.

Because Garry spoke English and French as well as his native tongue, his services were sought when Isaac I. Stevens, the new territorial governor of Washington who also served as head of the northern survey for a projected railroad route, came into the Spokane area during 1853. Garry made himself useful to members of the party much of the time that Stevens was in the Spokane area. Of particular importance was the fact that Spokane Garry served as a pathmaker for Lieutenant John Mullan.

Territorial governor Isaac I. Stevens must have been impressed with Garry, both as a Christian and guide, because he spent most of his diary entry of October 17, 1853 telling about his ability.

In the latter area, Garry informed a member of Steven's party "that there is a good trail from Spokane House to the Yakima country—"[21]

Stevens described Garry's home, which at that time was located near Spokane House site. His words read as follows:—"We found Garry's family in a comfortable lodge, and he informed us that he always had on hand flour, sugar and coffee, with which he could make his friends comfortable.[22]

Governor Stevens wrote under date of October 17, 1853 that Garry "Has an extensive field, where he raises a large quantity of wheat. Tomorrow he is going to Colville to get some of it ground."[23]

Later, when Stevens was recapping what had happened to various elements of his surveying party he explained:—

I had not mentioned in the proper place that when I parted with Garry the Spokane Chief at Vancouver [for he was also the guest of Colonel Bonneville][24] I made arrangements for him to express letters to Lieutenant Mullan, at Fort Owen, and in return to bring me news of

19

the operations of his party, and again in January, I also dispatched Higgins, who had been our wagon and pack master, with an express to the same point . . . . I had another object in pushing foreward those expresses which was to determine the depth of snow, from time to time, through the winter along the line of Clark's Fork, and thence to Cantonment Stevens, in the Bitterroot Valley. On the 6th of March Garry reached Olympia, with Lieutenant Mullan's report of his trip to Fort Hall and back in November and January. These trips caused him and his party to travel over 990 miles and to cross the divide of the Rocky mountains six times—three crossings have been made in the month of December and one in the month of January.''[25]

Mullan was searching for a route that could be used in winter when Garry and Higgins were sent from Olympia to Fort Hall. Harry found that the "greatest depth of snow found in the latter part of December and early in January on the route was one foot." Higgins made the trip in March and found no difficulty in traveling over the entire route.[26]

This skill added another dimension to Garry's accomplishments.

In his diary entry for Saturday, June 30, 1854, John Owen, sub-Indian agent at Fort Owen near present Stevensville, Montana, wrote that he had "a Visit from Spokan Garry." No further comment was made that would tell why Garry visited Owen but this entry locates where Garry was at this time.[27]

In 1855, Governor Isaac I. Stevens negotiated a treaty with the Yakima, Umatilla, Cayuse and Nez Perce Indians. The terms of the treaty were upsetting to the Indians and as a result of their dissatisfaction a short vicious war was fought.

Garry was at the treaty grounds in Walla Walla and spoke out for his tribe and others in the Spokane area.

Stevens promised Garry that he would hold a council with the Spokanes and their neighbors at a later time.

He proved his good faith by sending A.J. Bolon, the Yakima Indian agent, and a few men, to handle them, with some trade goods. These goods were to be stored there for safekeeping.

Bolon was told to inspect the Yakima reservation "then proceed to the Dalles and bring the Nez Perce Indian goods to Walla Walla, deposit them, and loading up with the Spokane goods, take them to Antoine Plante's ranch on the Spokane River, in readiness for the council on the governor's return from the Blackfoot country.''[28]

Had this projected treaty been negotiated there might not have been so many problems over Spokane lands as there ultimately was.

It is my understanding that Spokane Garry told Bolon that a party of Yakimas had slain some miners in the Yakima country and when he went to investigate the problem he was murdered by Qualchen, the son of Owhi, and others. This tragedy was a major cause for the war that took place during the years 1855-1856.[29]

Commissioner J.W. Denver, on November 30, 1857 in a letter to the Secretary of the Interior, gave some very clear reasons why the Indian outbreak took place in the Spokane and Coeur d'Alene country. He warned that there was danger of further war, one year before it happened. His reasons were:—

> The non-ratification of the treaties heretofore made to extinguish their title to the lands necessary for the occupancy and use of our citizens, seems to have produced no little disappointment, and the continued extension of our settlements into their territory, without any compensation being made to them, is a constant source of dissatisfaction and hostile feelings.[30] They are represented as being willing to dispose of their lands to the government, and I know of no alternative to the present unsatisfactory and dangerous state of things but the adoption of early measures for the extinguishment of their title, and their colonization on properly-located reservations, using and applying the consideration agreed to be allowed to them for their lands to sucsist (*sic*) and slothe them until they can be taught and influenced to support and sustain themselves.[31]

You will note on page 77 of the main text of this book, that Spokane Garry laid out some simple specifications for a move to a reservation for himself and his people.

It is evident that his simple demands were not met although they were well within the suggestions and limits made by J.W. Denver, the Commissioner of Indian Affairs.

It would not be unreasonable to assume that Spokane Garry was instrumental in persuading his people not to join the warring factions because in a letter from Isaac I. Stevens to Jefferson Davis, the Secretary of War, dated July 7, 1856, the governor wrote:—

"Kamiaken, at a council held with the Spokanes on the 25th May, wherein he urged that tribe to join the war, received a negative to his proposition."[32]

There was an uneasy peace for two years which was followed by two campaigns during the year 1858. One took place on May 17th, during which Lt. Col. Edward Jenner Steptoe, was soundly defeated by the allied tribesmen around and in the limits of the present confines of the town of Rosalia, Washington; and another, during which there were two battles; the first at Four Lakes and the second, on Spokane Plains, west of Spokane, Washington, during which the allied tribesmen were soundly beaten.

William S. Lewis describes these battles fully in this book.[33]

Most accounts agree that Spokane Garry tried to deter his tribesmen from participating in the war although Col. George Wright, at the meeting near the Mission Street bridge in Spokane, Washington, seemed to ignore this fact and blamed Garry for his tribe's activities during the campaign.

Garry helped Col. Wright as much as he could, because he brought some of his key people in, for talks, as well as to the treaty site later on Latah Creek. This is handled more fully in the main text.

John E. Smith, who was a trooper during the campaign, wrote about Garry when he came to the camp at the ford crossing. "Colonel Wright camped here a couple of days. Several Indians crossed ford and came into camp; among these was Spokane Garry. Garry was dressed in white man's clothes."

It was reported among the men that he hadn't taken any part in the fighting against the soldiers. He always had free access to the camp whenever he came to it—.[34]

The subject of our book seems to have obtained some money through government sources as explained by B.F. Yantis, a pioneer of Colville Valley, in a letter to Governor Stevens dated June 17, 1857

> A Mr. Wolf, a trader in this valley, has an order drawn by Garry for More than One thousand Dollars. Mr. W. has advanced him some four hundred Dollars on the Order. Now if the Government Owes Garry any More than will pay mr. W. advancement. I would be extremely glad to get some of it as they justly Owe me the amt of my claim & I Know now of no other way of getting it. He Garry leaves ere long for the Blackfoot Country on a war trip against the Snakes. If his sallary is still going on you had as well stop it as he of no avail to me.—[35]

John Owen's diary entry of April 24, 1860 informs us that he "...had a visit from Spokane Garry. Made a March of Seven Hrs. & Camped at a Small Lake. Spokane Garry joined Me this Morning and accompanies Me as far as Snake river as guide. We are Now on the battle ground of the four Lakes fought by Col. Wrights Command August 58."[36]

On June 1, 1859, a party of scientists set out from Kingston, Ontario, Canada under the leadership of Col. W.H. Nobles, to ascertain whether a road from St. Paul, Minnesota to the Pacific Northwest would be feasible. One member of his party was Dr. A.J. Thibodo, an amateur scientist, who kept a diary of their trip across the country. After a harrowing trip they reached Antoine Plante's place on the Spokane River on November 25th without provisons and upon arrival were fed by their host.

After buying some flour and horses with which to continue on their way, Thibodo hired Spokane Garry to guide his party to the Dalles, Oregon. He planned to leave the morning of November 26th but was delayed because "the Indian Chief Spokane Garry got drunk and could not go—so their start was delayed."

On a cold hazy Sunday morning a party of fifteen left the Plante place and headed for Walla Walla.

The above is another example of the chief's misuse of alcohol.[37]

While John Mullan was seeking a route through the Bitterroot Mountains in the winter for his military road, he learned that snow fell to a depth of two and a half to three feet in the Upper Coeur d'Alene and St. Regis Valleys but that Spokane Garry, who was carrying mail to and from the present Missoula area, was getting through by another route without too much trouble. Mullan's comments are as follows "During the winter of 1859, Spokane Garry brought the mail by way of the Clark's Fork, and though he lost one horse enroute, yet he nevertheless made the trips mostly on horseback."[38]

Mullan later learned that Indians used the Clark's Fork route in winter but did not use the Coeur d'Alene route because of deep snow.[39]

Spokane Garry was a mail man during this phase of his life.

In an article entitled "Pioneer Reminiscences," Thomas B. Beall told about his participation in building a bridge for Joe Herrin and Tim Lee across the Spokane River at the state line between Idaho and Washington. "The Indians came around occasionally while we were building the bridge. . . . I saw Chief Garry frequently that winter and spring (1864-1865) while we were building the bridge. He was pretty well fixed and then talked very good English. He wanted Herrin and Lee to pay him a bonus for the right to construct a bridge there. Garry was the leading chief of the Spokane Indians . . . ."[40]

[Ed. note] To the best of my knowledge Spokane Garry was attempting to obtain tribute from Herrin and Lee under false pretenses because the bridge was being built on Coeur d'Alene tribal lands and not Spokane lands. Spokane Bridge is well within the boundaries of Coeur d'Alene Indian lands as described on page 54 in my book *A Brief History of the Coeur d' Alene Indians* which was published by Ye Galleon Press in 1982, so Garry was trying to get money from the bridge builders through sheer bluff!

During the summer of 1878 Major-general O.O. Howard told his aide, Captain Melville Wilkinson,[41] to join Colonel E.C. Watkins, the Indian Inspector to meet several bands of allied natives in a council to be held at Spokane Falls.[42]

As many members of the following tribes as could be gathered together were assembled. There were three to four thousand present for the councils. Upper and Lower Spokanes, Okanogans, representations of the _____ and Colvilles all assembled to hear what was said. Spokane Garry was thought to be "more of a lawyer than a fighter" during the proceedings and according to General Howard he filibustered a long while in order to make a point.[43]

Howard noted that "His own band did not exceed three hundred but he hoped to increase his importance by having several bands collected and placed by the government under his leadership."[44]

Howard observed that "Spokane Garry was short in stature, dressed in citizens clothing, and wore his hair cut short for an Indian. He was shriveled, blear-eyed, and repulsive in appearance, but wiry and tough and still able to endure great fatigue, though he must have been at least seventy years of age."[45]

Howard also wrote that "The results of the council at Spokane Falls were quite satisfactory. All the renegades and Spokanes off from reservations secured from Colonel Watkins the promise of new and ample reservation, with metes and bounds well defined, and in return for this promise they agreed to keep the peace during the threatened Indian troubles whose shadow was already upon us."[46]

The entire text of this most interesting council may be found in the Report of the Secretary of War, Washington; Government Printing Office, 1877, pages 644 through 654.

Mrs. J.J. Brown told in a conversational manner that an attempt was made to place the Spokanes on a reservation in 1879. To quote her, "It was while we were still living in a very primitive way at the new place[47] in the early summer of 1879 that we entertained General O.O. Howard, who had come to the Falls to hold a meeting with the Indians in the effort to induce them to go on the reservation."

Spokane Garry was interested in placing his tribe on a reservation but his demands were for lands in and around the settlement of Spokane Falls or on the Little Spokane River and because of this his demands were never met.

He was at odds with the Peone branch of the Upper Spokanes because they were Catholic and he was an Episcopalian. He would not move onto the reservation that was given to the Spokane tribe because they were Presbyterians and he thought they were too Calvanistic. He would not go on the Coeur d'Alene reservation because they too were Catholics.

An early day pioneer described Garry's home "as a log shack with a roof of bull-rush matting laid over poles."[48]

There have been misconceptions about Garry's removal from the home east of Hillyard at Garry Spring, but that has been explained to the satisfaction of all. A very thorough job of research along with documentation should close that chapter forever. All of this excellent data can be found in pages 94 through 101, under the chapter heading "Schuyler Deloam Doak" and may be located in the book entitled *Orchard Prairie* by Kathryn Treffry Highberg, printed by Ye Galleon Press, Fairfield, Washington. 1978.

Once again this proves that Garry was in a manner his own worst enemy because he did not take advantage of the various offers made to him of moves to neighboring reservations.

It is obvious that he would not be given a reservation close to Spokane Falls and it was unlikely that he would be given further compensation for lands taken away from him over and above the moneys already given through the terms of the Spokane Indian treaty of 1887.

For an account of the negotiations at that time see Jerome Peltier *A Brief History of the Coeur d'Alene Indians 1806-1909,* Ye Galleon Press, Fairfield, Washington. 1982, pages 54 through 58.

After Garry was removed from his place near Hillyard, he and some of his people moved to Latah Creek Canyon. It was a poor location because some young juvenile delinquents of that day rolled rocks down on the villagers below. It became such an annoyance that Garry moved to Indian Canyon at the invitation of Gavin C. Mouat.

It was here that Spokane Garry died, January 14, 1892. William S. Lewis has written an excellent account of his end, but I would like to add a few words from a man who was an eye-witness of his death.

It was my good fortune to have had the opportunity to interview Ignace Hayden Garry, the great-grandson of Spokane Garry, who spent his childhood years in the tepee of the old chief and who was with him during his final illness.

During an interview October 12, 1961, Ignace said:—

When Grandma [Nelly Garry] brought me to school, she told that teacher I was a Garry. I'm not a Garry. I'm a Hayden. My grandfather was the man they named Hayden Lake after.

I knew Mouat. He lived on the hill above Indian Canyon and was with great-grandfather when he died. Others say he died later on, but I know he died January 2, 1892.

Before great-grandfather died he was sick.

There was a log laying there in front of the teepee(*sic*). They helped great-grandfather out of his place because he was so sick and weak. They wanted to take his picture with three or four of us boys, Alec Peone, Ellis Phillip, and Red Antelope [Silas, I think Old man Lowly].

One time I rode up the canyon with him after horses. He saw a ground hog go into his hole. He got a stick and stuck it down the hole. He must have got it into the skin of the ground hog because he twisted the stick around until he brought it (the animal) out of the hole twisted around the end of the stick. I never saw that done before. (Here Ignace changes the subject.) I don't know where the old school was but the Spokane's camped above the spring on the hill and below the spring. (Here Ignace means the school at Drumheller spring.)

(Ignace added) I moved from Indian Canyon to Worley in 1894.

As a parting note, I would like to interject the comments made by Ignace Garry during another taped interview, about Spokane Garry's death. "We lived on a creek. There was a little falls there. We lived in our tepee there. A log was there where Garry had his picture taken. I was five or six years old. I was there when he died. Some people from town came in a bobsled and took him to town. We rode in the bobsled."

With these few cryptic remarks I end my introduction and hope it will shed additional light on areas of Garry's life that are not covered in the excellent text that follows.

As I wrote these pages of additional data on Garry's life I could not feel that Garry needed an apology for his life because although he made mistakes, who hasn't. His virtues far outweighed his faults. I hope you judge him the same way as I did.

Jerome Peltier

LOWER FALLS OF THE SPOKANE (looking northeast)
Photograph taken about 1880 from a point beneath the present concrete bridge at Monroe Street.

FOOTNOTES FOR JEROME PELTIER INTRODUCTION

1   Frederick Merk. *Fur Trade and Empire*. Page 135.

2   *Ibid*. page 138.

3   Simon McGillivry entered the service of the North West Company as a clerk about 1803. He was in the Athabaska department of the company for several years. He was made a partner in the company prior to it's coalition with the Hudson's Bay Company in 1821. He was made a chief trader in 1821 after that union. He spent many years at Hamilton Inlet on the Labrador coast. In 1839 he was ordered to return to the Athabaska district and while enroute he died. He was married to Theresa Roy and they had nine children; four boys and five girls.

4   Burt Brown Barker. *Letters of John McLoughlin*. Page 293.

5   Lawrence Kip. *Army Life on the Pacific*. Page 70.

6   Elkanah Walker was one of the missionaries among the Spokane Indians from 1838-1848, at Tschimakain near present Ford, Washington. For a more complete account, read *Nine Years with the Spokane Indians* by Clifford M. Drury, as listed in the bibliography.

7   Tschimakain was the native name for the mission near present Ford, Washington.

8   Walker's Diary, page 175.

9   Same source.

10   Ibid. pages 242-243.

11   As above page 245.

12   Henry Harmon Spalding was the missionary at Lapwai, Idaho during the years 1836-1848. He later returned to the scene of his earlier endeavors during the 1870's. Read Clifford M. Drury—*The Diaries of Henry Harmon Spalding and Asa Bowen Smith,* for further information.

13   William H. Gray Journal, 1836-1837, page 20.

14   *Ibid*. page 75.

15   W.P. Winans. *Stevens County, It's Creation, Addition, Subtraction and Division*. Page 27. A copy of this very valuable historical account is in the editor's library as well as in the library of Cowles Museum.

16   George Simpson. *Journey Round the World*. Volume 1, pps. 144-145. Simpson seems to have expected too much of Garry because it is a well known fact that nearly all tribes of American Indians love to play the stick game. You will note that Simpson blamed American fur traders for introducing card games to the players. This is not necessarily true. You will also remember that Simpson did not write that Garry was actually playing cards but he was condemning him for introducing it to

29

his friends who were playing.

17 I neglected to ask Christine if she was talking about Garry Spring east of Hillyard or Drumheller Spring. Sorry!

18 Clifford M. Drury. *Diaries and Letters of Henry H. Spalding and Asa Bowen Smith.* Page 321.

19 *Ibid.* page 351

20 Clifford M. Drury. *First Women Over the Rockies.* Vol. 2, page 289.

21 R.R. Reports. Volume 12, book 1, pages 135 and 136.

22 *Ibid.* page 148.

23 Same source, page 136.

24 B.L.E. Bonneville was a native of France and his father, who was in trouble with the government, made arrangements for him to come to the United States secretly with his mother. They were accompanied by Thomas Paine, who used his influence to get Bonneville an appointment to West Point. He accompanied Lafayette while he was on his tour of the States in 1825. He was stationed on the frontier, and soon became interested in the fur trade. As a result he asked for two years leave of absence from the service while he pursued that career. He was given the leave on condition that he obtain information regarding the natives, and possible economic and geographic information he could obtain. It was to be financed by Bonneville at no expense to the government.

He began his operations at Fort Osage near Independence, Missouri May 1, 1832. He built Fort Bonneville on Green River, which was a great mistake because of the intemperate weather there during the winter. His wanderings were many, and among other things he was the first to bring wagons through South Pass.

He overstayed his pass, but was forgiven and reinstated into the service because of his contributions to knowledge of the west.

He served in the Seminole War and in the Mexican War. He was brevetted as Lieutenant Colonel because of injury in the latter war. In 1853 he was in command of Vancouver Barracks and mapped the military reservation there. He was loyal to the Union during the Civil War at which time he was made a Brevet Brigadier General.

He passed away at Fort Smith on June 12, 1878.

Washington Irving wrote about Bonneville's experiences in the fur trade in 1837.

25 *Ob. Sit.* R.R. Reports. Page 168.

26 As above, page 172.

27 Dunbar and Phillips. *The Journals and Letters of Major John Owen, 1850-1871.* 2 Volumes, Edward Eberstadt, N.Y., 1927. Volume 1, page 105. Hereafter to be named Owen Journals.

28 Hazard Stevens. *Life of Isaac I. Stevens.* 2 Volumes, page 67.

29 A complete account of the killing of Bolon may be found in a booklet written by L.V. McWhorter entitled *The Tragedy of the Wahk-Shum.*

30 The treaty of 1855 was not radified by Congress until 1859. Is it any wonder that the Indians thought they were being double crossed?

31 *Report of the Commissioner of Indian Affairs*, 1857, page 299.

32 *Message of the Governor of Washington Territory*, 1857, page 83.

33 For further study of this interesting phase of Spokane Indian history, you may wish to consult *Warbonnets and Epaulets* by Jerome Peltier; *Conquest of the Spokanes, Coeur d'Alenes and Palouses* by B.F. Manring and *Indian Side of the Story* by William C. Brown.

34 John E. Brown. *A Pioneer of Spokane.* Pages 269 and 270.

35 *Pacific Northwest Quarterly.* October 1940, page 415. Francis Wolf was also the sheriff of the Colville area.

36 *Owen's Journal.* Volume 1, page 212.

37 *Pacific Northwest Quarterly.* July 1940, page 339.

38 John Mullan. Report page 19.

39 *Ibid.* Page 19.

40 Thomas B. Beall. *Pioneer Reminiscences.* Washington Historical Quarterly, April 1917, pages 86 and 87.

41 Melville Cary Wilkinson, a native of New York, entered West Point from N.Y. Served in various positions during the Civil War and was mustered out of service June 30, 1866. He was brevetted 1st Lt. the 2nd of March 1867 for gallant and meritorious service in the Battle of Antietam, Md.; Captain 2nd March, 1867 for gallant and meritorious service during the war; Major 27th February, 1890 for gallant service in action against Indians at Kamiah, Idaho 13th July, 1877. He was killed in action on October 5, 1898 by Indians at Bear Island, Leach Lake, Minnesota. Heitman, *Historical Register of the Army*, Volume 1, page 1037.

42 O.O. Howard. *My Life and Experiences etc.* Page 434.

43 *Ibid.* Page 435.

44 Same source, page 435.

45 As above, page 435.

46 Same source, page 435.

47 Their home was in the present Brown's Addition of Spokane. The area was named for them.

48 Kathryn Treffry Highberg. *Orchard Prairie.* Ye Galleon Press, Fairfield, Washington, 1978, page 20.

LOWER FALLS OF THE SPOKANE RIVER AS THEY APPEARED
IN THE 1870'S.
Photograph taken from a point near the east end of the
present Post Street Bridge.

INTRODUCTION

The remains of Spokane Garry, Chief of the Spokane Indians, are buried in a neglected spot in the southern part of Greenwood Cemetary, near Indian Canyon, in the City of Spokane. Chief Garry was one of the human links connecting the history of Spokane House, the old fur trading post, with that of the present City of Spokane. He was born about 1811 (some authorities indicate about 1813[1]), a year after Jacques Raphael Finlay, a clerk of the Northwest Company of Merchants of Canada, erected the first trading post at Spokane, and a year prior to the arrival of the Astor party under the command of John Clark. The place of his birth was probably the main camp of the Spokane Indians on the level point of land at the junction of the Spokane and Little Spokane Rivers, in the vicinity of which both trading posts were erected, and about nine miles northwest from the present City of Spokane.

The life of Spokane Garry shows a remarkable advance from savagery to education and civilization, through the influence of the early fur traders and first missionaries; a progress unhappily checked and thwarted by acts and conduct of later settlers and government official, which forced the Chief, in his old age, to return to the nomadic tent life of his fathers.

The story is in some respects a pathetic one. The influences wielded by Garry over his one-time numerous tribe enabled the whites gradually to possess themselves of the broad acres formerly the pasture lands for immense bands of Indian ponies, until at last the Spokanes were crowded out of the territory which their forefathers had from time immemorial possessed. Having been overlooked when the various neighboring tribes were allotted to reservations, Garry and his people, driven at last from their homes by covetous homesteaders, found themselves wanderers on the face of the earth; blown hither and yonder by the winds of adversity; regarded as a nuisance wherever they chanced to stay, and tolerated only when it was impossible to compel them to further pilgrimage. They have seen cities spring up where once their tepees were erected, and have watched the construction of railroads over the plains and through the canyons where their ponies formerly bore them safely. Their hunting grounds have been transformed into wheat fields, and their pasture lands into orchards, and in all the change and prosperity that has followed the advent of the white man they have had no part, except to drift further and further into vagabondage. Their numbers have steadily decreased until a few remain of a once numerous tribe, and the time is not far distant when they will be a memory only.[2] They have become exiles from the place of their birth, and with a few exceptions, the remaining Spokane Indians are now scattered on the Flathead Reservation in Montana, the Coeur d'Alene Reservation in Idaho, and the Spokane and Colville Reservations in Washington.

While the coming of the first white men (the fur traders and first missionaries) was an incalculable benefit to the Indians in that it furnished them with arms and equipment to kill game, tools and utensils with which to cook and live, flint and steel for their fires, and cloth and blankets for protection against the elements, seeds and tools for the cultivation of fields and gardens, and a superior code of ethics and religion for the guidance of their lives, candor compels me to state that the influx of the later settlers was not an unmixed blessing to the Indians. ''They had been taught by their spiritual guides to esteem the sublime doctrines of Christianity, doctrines which demand from their adherents the exercise of charity, purity, temperance; on the other hand, they saw in the conduct of many white settlers a flagrant contradiction to these doctrines—the occupation of lands once owned by them gave rise to a spirit of discontent and to a lack of confidence in the doctrines they had been taught to hold sacred. Sickness, too, brought on principally by the sudden change of life forced on them by necessary contact with the white population, hastened to bring on that decadence whose end we see today.''[3]

Two score and more years have now elapsed since the first strenuous days of pioneer settlement in the Spokane County, and it has occurred to the writer that the present generation may be in a sufficiently tolerant and indulgent mood to recognize and appreciate the few homely virtues and the modest accomplishments of old Chief Garry.

FOOTNOTES TO INTRODUCTION

1   Curtis, *North American Indian*, Vol. VII, p. 55.

2   *The Spokesman* (Spokane, Washington), January 14, 1892, p. 6.

3   *Gonzaga Silver Jubilee Memoir*, p. 19.

Chief Spokane Garry's hymnal and pipe. Courtesy of Richard T. Lewis.

SPOKANE GARRY
Sketch made by George Schon (Gustavus Sohon) at the Walla
Walla Indian Council, May 27, 1855.

PART I

THE FACTS IN THE CASE

CHAPTER I

GARRY'S EARLY LIFE

The name of Spokane Garry's mother has not been preserved. His father was the head chief of the Sin-ho-man-naish Indians and known by the name of Illim-Spokanee'[1]—Child of the Sun and the Moon. When the first white man came into the Northwest the Spokane Indians were not known by that name, but were known by the Indian names of the localities where the respective tribes lived: as the Sin-sla-quish, afterwards called the Coeur d'Alenes by the French fur traders; the Sin-too-too-oulish or Muddy Creek people, afterwards called the Upper Spokanes; and the Sin-ho-man-naish—the salmon trout people—afterwards called the Middle Spokanes by the white men. The chief men of the Sin-ho-man-naish tribe at the beginning of the last century were two brothers, one called Chief Child of the Sun and the Moon—Illim-Spokanee', and the other called Chief Daylight—Hulholt. In those days the Sin-ho-man-naish were a large and powerful tribe, and the head chief, Illim-Spokanee', was known and respected over a considerable portion of the "old Oregon" country. The first explorers and fur traders gave the name of this head chief, Illim-Spokanee', to the tribe, to the river, and to the country which they inhabited. The name "Spokane" is thus the name of the head chief (Garry's father) and was not originally the name of either

37

the people, the river, or the country.[2]

At the time of the arrival of the Astor enterprise, Garry's father was an old man. Ross Cox in his book (Volume 1, page 180) refers to the old chief as "a harmless old man who spent a great portion of his time between us (the Astor post)[3] and McMillan's (the Northwest post)." Garry's early boyhood was probably spent at the big Indian camp in the vicinity of the trading posts and at the various camping grounds of the tribe along the Spokane River and the neighboring lakes and plains. He had an older brother named Sultz-lee and a sister named Quint-qua-a'pee—there were other children whose names are not known.

In 1821 the great Hudson Bay Company succeeded to the fur business of the Northwest Company, which had taken over the Astor enterprise at Spokane and elsewhere in the Columbia District in 1813; and, in 1825, Governor George Simpson,[4] who had general charge of the affairs of the Hudson Bay Company west of the Rocky Mountains, conceived the idea of selecting a number of Indian boys from the various Columbia River tribes and sending them to be educated at the Red River Colony,[5] east of the mountains, Governor Simpson's idea being that, on their return, they could aid in the civilization of their respective tribes.

Alexander Ross,[6] an old Astor company employee who had remained in the country in the employ of the different fur companies, was directed by Governor Simpson to select two of these boys, and he made request of the Spokane and Kootenai tribes that they each furnish a candidate from their respective tribes. It is a striking proof of the great confidence which the ignorant savages placed in the white men, that, notwithstanding their reluctance to part with their children, none of whom had ever left their native country before, after a council or two had been held, the chiefs of the Spokane and Kootenai tribes not only complied with the request, but as a more striking example of their trust, agreed to let two of their own children go, and turned them over to Mr. Ross unhesitatingly. The council being over, the father of one of the boys arose and said to

Ross: "You see, we have given you our children, not our servants, or our slaves, but our own," and striking at the same time one hand on his left breast, while pointing with the other to his wife, the mother of the boy, he continued, "We have given you our hearts—our children are our hearts—but bring them back again to us before they become white men. We wish to see them once more Indians, and after that you can make them white men if you like. But let them not get sick or die. If they get sick, we shall get sick; if they die, we shall die. Take them, they are now yours." When the old chief sat down, all present broke out in lamentations, after which the two chiefs again rose, and placing their boys' hands in Ross' hand, silently departed.[7]

HOW GARRY GOT HIS NAME

The son of the Spokane chief was now named Spokane Garry, after his tribe, and Garry,[8] one of the directors of the Hudson Bay Company; while the son of the Kootenai chief was named Kootenai Pelly, after his tribe, and Governor Pelly[9] of the Hudson Bay Company. Both boys were fine, promising youths of equal age, and were the brightest and most intelligent of their respective tribes. They left Spokane with the brigade on the 12th of April, 1825, in company with governor Simpson, Chief Trader McMillan, Alexander Ross, his son, and fifteen men,[10] and ascending the Columbia in canoes to Boat Encampment at the mouth of Canoe River, crossed the Rocky Mountains and proceeded overland to the Red River Settlement. Spokane Garry and Kootenai Pelly, with six[11] other Indian youths, were educated in the Red River Missionary School, and were the first Indians belonging to the Oregon country that were ever taught to read and write. After making considerable progress in learning, Kootenai Pelly took sick and died.

Spokane Garry spent five years in the Red River Settlement, and secured a good education, learning to speak and to read and write both English and French, and acquiring some of the veneer, and accustoming himself to the refinements of civilized life.

David Douglas, the Scotch botanist, after whom the Douglas fir was named, and who spent part of the year 1826 in the Spokane country, states in his journal, recently published, that when he reached Fort Garry in 1827 on his return from the Columbia River district, Spokane Garry, who was then attending the missionary school, called on him and enquired about his father and brothers, whom Douglas had recently seen. Douglas remarks that Garry spoke good English and had nearly forgotten his mother tongue (Spokane).[12]

GARRY RETURNS HOME

Garry returned to the Spokane country in 1830 after an absence of five years, and was, henceforth, prominently connected with all matters relating to Indian affairs in this section; he rapidly acquired influence among the Spokane and neighboring Indians, and was for sixty years the leading Indian character of the Spokane country, and the champion of the Spokane Indians in councils with the whites, with whom he ever maintained friendship.

To use the language of Curley Jim, a contemporary, "The chiefs of the various tribes liked Garry very well." Soon after his return from the Red River country they made him a chief and gave him two wives—one a Umatilla, the other a San Poil.[13] The first wife, Nina, was Garry's favorite and lived in the upper Spokane country about Newman, Liberty and Saltese Lakes and what is now known as Peone and Pleasant Prairies; the other wife lived in the lower Spokane country, near the Columbia River. By these two wives Garry had nine children: Susie, Jim Crow, Lucy, Ben, Koosai, Nellie, and three others who died when very young. Of the two wives, Nina survived Chief Garry and died only a few years ago on the Coeur d'Alene Reservation. Of the children, two only survive, Nellie, a daughter of Nina, at present living on the Coeur d'Alene Reservation, and Ok-Pee, or Lucy, a daughter of the San Poil wife, living on the Spokane Reservation.[14]

SPOKANE GARRY WAS THE FIRST CHRISTIAN MISSIONARY AMONG HIS PEOPLE, THE
SPOKANE INDIANS

Previous to Spokane Garry's return from the Red River
Missionary School, the sole knowledge possessed by the Spokane
Indians of the white man's religion was confined to what little they
had learned from their intercourse with the fur traders. Garry seems
to have returned home with some high ideals for the enlightenment
of his tribe. Soon after his return he commenced to give the Indians
their first religious instruction. Curley Jim states that Garry taught
the Indians not to steal and not to kill. "He told us of a God up
above. Showed us a book, the Bible, from which he read to us. He
said to us, if we were good, that then when we died, we would go up
above and see God. After Chief Garry started to teach them the
Spokane Indians woke up. Chief Garry used to read to them from his
Bible. Nellie, Garry's daughter, has the Bible."[15]

Speaking on the same subject, Nellie says: "Garry read the
Bible to the Indians. I have Chief Garry's Bible. My father taught me
how to pray; taught me a morning and an evening prayer; taught me
my first religion." After Garry commenced to preach, people from
other tribes came to hear him, and his influence was extended.

The old Indians of the tribe say that there was not much
difference between Spokane Garry's teachings and that of the later
missionaries. He first taught the Indians the Ten Commandments,
and then proceeded to teach them from his little book (*Minor
Historical Catechism*). Garry's method was to first show the Indians
the pictures at the commencement of each lesson, and then read and
explain to them the accompanying lesson. Sometimes when Spokane
Garry was absent the older Indians who were familiar with the pictures
and knew the respective lessons, held the meetings in Garry's stead.
Religious services were held at least every Sunday, and the Indians
came from the Colville, Nez Perce, Okanogan and Flat Head tribes to
hear Garry. This teaching was commenced by him several years before
the arrival of the first Protestant and Catholic missionaries.[16]

On the evening of May 27, 1836, near Loon Lake, the Rev. Samuel Parker of Ithaca, New York, on his way from Fort Walla Walla to Fort Colville, the Hudson Bay post on Marcus Flats, held a public worship for a number of Spokane and Nez Perce Indians. Spokane Garry acted as interpreter for the Spokanes and a Nez Perce chief who understood the Spokane language, translated the sermon into Nez Perce. Mr. Parker states that Garry was a good interpreter and had a very good knowledge of English.[17]

In March 1837, W.H. Gray, the associate of Dr. Marcus Whitman, came to the Spokane country and met here the Rev. Henry H. Spaulding, who was then on his way to Fort Colville, the Hudson Bay trading post. Mr. Gray states that Chief Garry had induced his tribe to erect a house for religious services of sufficient size to hold all the people in the village, and that Garry, with his Bible, was making an effort to teach the Spokane Indians the rudiments of the Christian religion.[18]

The visit of Rev. Samuel Parker on May 27, 1836 and that of Messrs. Gray and Spaulding led to the establishment of the mission on Walker's Prairie in 1838. Nellie Garry states that, having learned about the white man's religion from her father, the Indians liked the white missionaries very well.[19]

The efforts of Spokane Garry to convert his tribe seem to have been somewhat unappreciated, but no more unprofitable than those of his two white brothers, the Rev. Elkanah Walker and the Rev. Cushing Eells, who conducted the neighboring missionary establishment on the Chimokaine, a few miles distant from Spokane House, and which they abandoned in June, 1848, after ten years of self-sacrificing effort. Mrs. Eells, writing in October, 1847, said that in nearly nine years they had not secured one convert. In a recent letter, Mr. Edwin Eells, a son, states that not a single professed convert was made during the entire ten years.

Spokane Garry himself gradually abandoned his efforts at religious teaching, and when pressed for the reason, gruffly stated that he had quit because the other Indians "jawed him so much about it."[20]

THE CASE OF SPOKANE GARRY

GARRY AND THE PROTESTANT MISSIONARIES

There does not appear to have been much co-operation between the Rev. Eells and Walker and Spokane Garry, and it is the personal impression of the writer that these self-sacrificing and devout missionaries were temperamentally incapable of a sympathetic understanding of the Indian character, or of fully availing themselves of Spokane Garry's services and previous efforts, or of successfully cultivating what has been stated to have been ''as fertile soil as could be found in the Northwest for the planting of Christian teachings.''[21]

The writer has not had an opportunity to examine all the accessible letters, journals and records of Messrs. Eells and Walker covering their life at Tschimokaine mission from 1838 to 1848, but so far as they have been examined by him, it does not appear that Spokane Garry visited their mission prior to 1841. The following appears in Mr. Walker's journal of that year:

Thursday 5. (January, 1841) The weather cloudy and cold without snow. Garry made his appearance for the first time since we have been here.

Saturday 15 (January, 1842) * * * * Garry came in tonight, had a long talk with him on the language and engaged him to rehearse as the teacher is sick.

Sunday 16. (January) Garry came up this morning quite early before Mr. E. went to worship and I had a long talk with him and received considerable information about the language. When the time of worship came he refused to rehearse and left me to my own resources.

*　　　　　*　　　　　*　　　　　*

Saturday 24. (Jan.) The express came in contrary to our expectations and with it Mr. Garry returned. Did not talk with him last night.

Sunday 25. (January) * * * * Mr. Eells talked with them (Indians) at noon. I had Garry interpret a part of what he said. He did it very well. I had G. come up after services and I went over a subject

43

for the third service. After I had done I called on Garry to say something. He was long in answering and began very low, saying that he was ashamed and how could he help it. * * * * I had thought considerable when listening to Garry to hear him pour the truth unto them, and when he illustrated the awful condition of the finally lost.

Wed. 9 (February, 1842) Have had a long talk with Garry on the language.

Sun. 13. Have been mostly on the Lord's prayer, as I have had it translated of late by Garry.

Thurs. 17. Had some talk with Garry about coming here and think that he will.

Wed. 30. Soon Garry made his appearance, I have had some conversation with him about coming here and found him very favorably disposed.

Friday, April 1 (1842) Just at night Garry came in.

Sat. 2 Gave Garry some wheat and potatoes for seed, and gave him part of an ox. He wanted to trade a small part of deer tallow for a shirt. I lent him two hoes. He wanted six. He may cause us much trouble, but we must learn him that we cannot give him all he wants.

Mon. 4. Had some talk with Garry on the language.

Thurs. 14. Garry left this morning and I have engaged an Indian for a while.

Thurs. 29. (June, 1842) Garry made a call today and said that he was going to Colville and thought that he would see Mr. E. (Eells).

The Rev. H.T. Cowley, who came as a missionary in 1874, says of Garry and his religious teachings:

When he first returned from the Red River District he was very zealous and attempted to instruct his tribesmen in the Christian religion. He called the Indians together in an Indian lodge or church with a bell and began to lay down the Christian tenets to them, attempting to hold them in rigid discipline and held Christian worship every morning and evening.[22] He was very zealous but the Indians did not seem to understand or appreciate his efforts, finally most of them repudiated him as a leader and teacher in religion.[23]

RIVALRY WITH THE JESUITS

Through the efforts of Spokane Garry and the Reverends Walker and Eells, many of the Spokane Indians had become Protestants. Their neighbors, the Coeur d'Alenes, among whom the early Jesuits settled, became Catholics, and when they met the Spokanes, taunted them as heretics whose faith was worthless. Mr. George Gibbs, who accompanied the government railroad surveyors in 1853, states that Chief Garry narrated to him, ''the evils arising from this state of feeling, with a forbearance and Christian spirit of toleration which would have honored anyone.''[24]

Between 1863 and 1866, Fathers Giorda, Caruana, Cataldo and Tosi invaded Garry's home precincts and commenced missionary work among the Spokane Indians. On December 8th, 1866, they held the first services in their mission, dedicated to St. Michael, established among the Upper Spokanes on Peone Prairie, about two miles north of the present locality of that name.

It seems that when Father Cataldo came to erect this mission Chief Garry was absent and some of the Spokane Indians demurred against assuming the responsibility of granting the Father license to erect the chapel in Garry's absence. The Father, however, proceeded with the building, saying that, if the Indians did not want to keep it, he would destroy it at the end of three months. With some murmurings, the Indians assented. At the end of three months, through the Father's zealous efforts, nearly half of the Upper Spokane Indians had become Catholics. Spokane Garry himself was a Presbyterian, and on his return he wanted the Catholic chapel moved or destroyed, but the Peones—one of the largest families of the tribe—and many others having become Catholic converts, they stated that they would not consent to Father Cataldo's leaving, or to the mission being destroyed, and that if Chief Garry did not like what had been done in his absence he could go elsewhere.[25]

Chief Garry, whose home was in the vicinity of the Catholic institution, and through whose exertions many of the Spokane

Indians had become Presbyterians, could not see without regret many of his tribe embracing the Catholic faith. He accordingly called for aid and had camp meetings and revival services held to counteract the missionary efforts of Fathers Giorda, Cataldo and Tosi, who responded by holding a mission of two weeks to the Spokanes, at which a number of new Catholic converts were made. Spokane Garry was defeated; most of the Upper Spokanes embraced the Catholic faith; and in the vicinity of the little St. Michael Mission there has since grown one of the largest institutions for the training of Catholic clergy in America.

Later, in 1873, a delegation of Spokane Indians was, at Garry's instigation, sent to the Rev. H.H. Spaulding at Kamia (*sic*), Idaho requesting him to visit them and hold revival services. Mr. Spaulding returned with the delegation and held services in the Spokane Valley, where two hundred and fifty-three Indians—some of whom had previously been baptized by Father Cataldo—were baptized and confirmed in the Protestant faith.[26]

CHIEF GARRY WAS THE FIRST SCHOOL TEACHER IN THE SPOKANE COUNTRY

When Spokane Garry returned from the Red River country, he undertook to conduct a school for the benefit of his countrymen. To this end he induced the Indians to construct a schoolhouse, 20 by 50 feet in size. This was built about two miles north of the Falls of Spokane, at the foot of the gravel terrace or bench, near a large spring, afterwards called Drumheller's Springs, west of Monroe Street, and now well inside the limits of the City of Spokane.[27] In early days one of the principal Indian trails passed this spot, and the site was a favorite camping ground of the Indians. On the gravel bench above was an extensive Indian burial ground now occupied by comfortable homes.

The schoolhouse was built with a framework of poles covered with tule mats. The reeds were woven and sewed together by the squaws into mats, which were stretched over the framework of the building. An early Spokane Indian church, described by Dr. Eells in the *Missionary Herald* of 1840,[28] was constructed in a similar manner. This school was conducted by Chief Garry during the winter months. Mr. W.H. Gray, author of *Gray's History of Oregon*, and an associate of Marcus Whitman, visited the school in April, 1837, and recorded in his journal that Garry was conducting a native school near Spokane House, and was attempting to teach the Indians to read and write English. Spokane Garry had to suspend his school occasionally, as the Indian children who attended it could not get enough to eat, and teacher and scholars were often reduced to a diet of sunflowers and roots. Many of Garry's scholars still survive: John Stevens, Charley Warren, Thomas Garry, etc.[29] Nellie Garry states that her father also taught his children to read and write English.

CHIEF GARRY WAS A FARMER; HE INSTRUCTED THE SPOKANE INDIANS IN AGRICULTURE

In addition to the instruction given at his school, Spokane Garry taught the Indians some things of a more practical nature. He encouraged them to raise gardens and fields of grain, and instructed them as to the best methods of agriculture, learned by him at the Red River Settlement.

The Spokane Indians had received their first knowledge of agriculture from the fur traders at Spokane House in 1813 and 1814. One of the clerks records that the fur traders had to keep a guard over their melon patch after the Indians had once sampled them. Having seen the traders plant and harvest their potatoes, grain and vegetables, and observed them afterwards cook and eat them, the Indians secured some seeds and commenced to raise some small gardens themselves. Chief Garry's efforts made the cultivation of gardens and fields common among his people.[30]

In 1837 Garry furnished the missionary, Henry H. Spaulding with a large quantity of seed potatoes and had a large and productive garden of roots and vegetables.[31] He also raised considerable wheat. This was threshed out on a wooden floor by turning in a bunch of Indian ponies to trample out the grain, which was then gathered in baskets and carried to Fort Colville, where it was ground into flour at the Hudson Bay grist mill, at what is now Meyers Falls.[32]

At the time of the arrival of Governor I.I. Stevens and party in 1853, Spokane Garry and many of his countrymen were raising fields of wheat, containing from five to thirty acres each, and gardens of potatoes, pumpkins, corn, squash and vegetables. At the time of the Indian War of 1858 many Indian granaries in the Spokane Valley, filled with wheat, were burnt and destroyed by command of Colonel Wright.[33] At this time Spokane Garry himself had a large crop of potatoes, wheat and vegetables; these, his daughter states, were given freely to both Indians and soldiers—to whoever needed them. In later years Spokane Garry frequently gave grain and small supplies of potatoes and vegetables to needy white settlers.[34] Later, at the time of the construction of the Northern Pacific Railroad in 1880 and 1881, Spokane Garry sold grain and vegetables from his farm by the pack load to the white men and Chinamen engaged in the railroad construction work.[35]

CHIEF GARRY PROMOTED THE FIRST FLOUR MILLING ENTERPRISE IN THE SPOKANE COUNTRY

The farming operations conducted by Spokane Garry and his tribesmen had grown so extensive by the latter 50's that a contract was made by Garry for the construction of a flour mill on the Little Spokane at In-chi-ten-see,[36] later known as Selheim Springs, and now a part of the country estate of Mr. J.P. Graves.

The terms of the contract are unknown. In 1859, B.F. Yantis, generally known as "Judge" Yantis, set out from Olympia with the grinding machinery for this little mill, and freighted it out to the site on the Little Spokane. A mill race and water wheel were constructed and the mill building completed and the machinery installed and operated for a short time, when some misunderstanding or disagreement occurred, and Judge Yantis took out his machinery and removed it to the Colville Valley, where he later set it up on the Little Pend Oreille River. This mill was later known as the Oppenheimer mill.

Chief Garry's side of the controversy is not known. Judge Yantis

48

related that Spokane Garry seemed to think that he (Yantis) couldn't carry his machinery further and repudiated his contract.[37] John Stevens and other Spokane Indians say that after the mill was in operation, the white man (Yantis) began to claim title to the Indian lands on which the mill had been built, whereupon the Indians, to extinguish any such claim, tore down the mill.[38]

SPOKANE GARRY AND HIS OLD WHITE HORSE
Photograph taken about 1880, near the old Indian camp below the falls, now "Peaceful Valley," in the heart of the City of Spokane, just north from the Spokane Public Library Building.

FOOTNOTES FOR CHAPTER I

1   Ignace Garry, last chief of the Coeur d'Alene tribe, said that his great-great-grandfather was known as Illim-eekum-Spokanee, which translated meant Child of the Sun and Moon.

2   Statements of Thomas Garry, *et al.*, Library of the Spokane Historical Society. See Symons' *Columbia River*, pp. 128, 129. Compare with Indian names as given by George Gibbs and Curtis, post page 24; Gaunett's *Origin of Certain Place Names in the United States*, p. 288, and *Handbook of American Indians*, Bulletin 30, p. 625, Bureau of American Ethnology; also *Henry Thompson Journals*, Vol. 2.

3   The "Astor Post" was Fort Spokan (1812-1814), an establishment of the Pacific Fur Company owned by John Jacob Astor. The Northwest post (1810-1826) was called Spokane House. Both posts were built close to each other at the confluence of the Spokane and Little Spokane Rivers.

4   George Simpson was a cousin of the explorer, Thomas Simpson. He went to the Athabasca department of the Hudson Bay Company from the London office in 1820. On the union of the North-West Company with the older company on March 26, 1821, he became junior governor of the company's territories and soon assumed practically sole supervision over the company's business in America. He was for 40 years prominent in the company's affairs. In 1839 he received knighthood, and in 1841 made a journey around the world, of which he published an entertaining account.

5   *Journey Around the World*, George Simpson, p. 130.

6   Alexander Ross was a Scotch school teacher and farmer, from Upper Canada. Attracted by the Astor enterprise, he enlisted as a clerk and sailed on the *Tonquin*. He was a member of the party establishing Fort Okanogan in 1811; remained on the Columbia in the employment of the North-West and Hudson Bay Companies until 1825, when he went to the Red River District. He died in 1858, and was the author of three books, two of them relating to the early history of the Northwest fur companies in the Columbia.

7   *Fur Traders*, Alex. Ross, Vol. 2, p. 157.

8   Nicholas Garry, deputy governor of the company, in whose honor Forts Garry on the Red River, Manitoba, were named; old or Lower Fort Garry, erected after the union of the two companies in 1821, and Upper or new Fort Garry, the erection of which was commenced at the forks of the Red River in 1855. This became the site of the present City of Winnipeg.

9   Sir John Henry Pelley—a cousin, Robert Parker Pelley, held a power of attorney with Governor Simpson from the Selkirk executors, and was associated with

Simpson in the Northwest.

10 *Fur Traders*, Alex. Ross, Vol. 2, p. 160.

11 I have been unable to ascertain the names of these youths, or the tribes they were selected from. Curley Jim, an intelligent Spokane Indian, states that Ellis and Jim Lion were sent from the Nez Perces and also a son of Ta-loom (Thunder), one of the Coeur d'Alene chiefs. He also states that all the boys came back. Spokane Garry seems to have been the only one of these Indians that attempted to use his education for the improvement of his tribe.

12 Journal of David Douglas, p. 280.

13 Statement of Curley Jim, Library Spokane Historical Society; U.S. (Wilkes) exploring expedition, Vol. 4, pp. 458-9. Garry was first chief of the Sin-homene, or Middle Spokanes; later he became in effect chief of the Sintutuuli or Upper Spokanes. Curtis, *North American Indian*, Vol. VII, p. 55. The Indian name sin-tu-tu-uli signifies the place where the little fish are caught.

14 Statement of Nellie Garry, Library Spokane Historical Society.

15 Statement of Curley Jim, *supra*.

16 Statement of Nellie Garry, *supra*. See Curtis, *North American Indian*, Vol. VII, p. 55. Statement of Thomas Garry, Moses Phillips, *et al.*

17 Parker's *Journal of an Exploring Tour*, etc., p. 289.

18 Wm. H. Gray's *Journal*, p. 77. In the copy of the diary of the Rev. E. Walker, in possession of the Oregon Historical Society, under date Saturday, September 15, 1838, recently read by me, there is a statement that at the camp of the missionaries on that date near the Indian village at old Spokane House, the Rev. Cushing Eells read to the Indians from the New Testament and that the Indians ''said that Gray had read the same.'' The writer is of the opinion that in copying from the original diary the name Gray has been erroneously inserted in place of Garry. Spokane Garry is known to have then been reading the Bible to the Indians for several years, and Gray himself mentions this in his journal of the only trip he made to the Spokane country prior to September 15, 1838, while Mr. Gray makes no mention of having himself read any religious services for the Indians. He came up from Walla Walla with Mr. Ermatinger, and at Spokane met the Rev. H.H. Spaulding. From Mr. Gray's journal it appears that the Rev. Spaulding did give the Spokane Indians some religious instruction on April 2, 1837, and that all the intercourse with the Indians was had by the Rev. Spaulding and none by Mr. Gray. See Gray's *Journal*, pp. 15, 16.

19 Statement of Nellie Garry, *supra*.

20 Letter of Mr. Edwin Eells, Library Spokane Historical Society. Simpson's *Journey Around the World*, p. 145.

21 Curtis' *North American Indian,* Vol. 7, p. 55.

22 Compare this with Elkanah Walker's diary under date Saturday, September 22, 1838.

23 Statement of Rev. H.T. Cowley. Mr. Cowley was for some time associated with the Rev. Spaulding at Kamia.

24 Gibb's report to McClellan, 1 Pac. Ry. Reports, p. 414.

25 *Gonzaga Silver Jubilee Memoir,* pp. 10-11. See also manuscript in the Library of the Spokane Historical Society; also statement of Thomas Garry, *et al.,* Library Spokane Historical Society.

26 *Gonzaga Silver Jubilee Memoir,* pp. 9-14. Whitman College Quarterly, Vol. 3, No. 3, p. 15. See also statement of Thomas Garry, *et al.*

27 Statement of Nellie Garry.

28 *Missionary Herald* of 1840, p. 437; Father Eells, p. 96.

29 Wm. H. Gray's *Journal,* pp. 15-17.l See also statement of Thomas Garry, *et al.,* Library Spokane Historical Society.

30 Gray's *History of Oregon,* p. 17, Parker's *Travels,* p. 288; Gray's *Journal,* pp. 15-16; Father Eells, p. 99; see *Pioneer Reminiscences,* Library Spokane Historical Society.

31 *Journal,* Wm. H. Gray, pp. 15-16.

32 Pac. Ry. Reports, Vol. 12, p. 136; also statement of Curley Jim.

33 Kipp's *Army Life on the Pacific,* p. 70.

34 *The Chronicle,* Spokane, Washington, January 14, 1892, p. 6.

35 Statement of Nellie Garry, *supra.*

36 Statements of Susan Michel, John Stevens and others, Library of Spokane Historical Society. In-chi-ten-see in the Spokane language signifies "the place where another little stream comes in."

37 Statement of W.P. Winans, Library of Spokane Historical Society. B.F. Yantis was a Kentuckian, born on March 19, 1807. He moved to the Pacific Coast in 1852 and occupied many positions of trust in Washington Territory, serving as a Justice of the Peace and Legislator. After the creation of Idaho Territory he resided there for some time and served in the Legislature of that Territory. He finally returned to the Sound, where he died in 1879.—Olympia (Wash.) *Standard,* February 15, 1879.

38 Statement of John Stevens, Library Spokane Historical Society.

CHAPTER II

SPOKANE GARRY AND THE STEVENS PARTY

n 1853, Governor Isaac I. Stevens and party reached the Spokane country, and in his report, written in the spring of 1854, Governor Stevens says:

"Garry, the Spokane Chief, is a man of education, of strict probity and great influence over his tribe. He speaks English and French well."[1] At another point in his report he states: "Garry is a man of judgment, forecast and great reliability. He has a comfortable lodge, and always has on hand flour, sugar and coffee."[2] At Governor Stevens' request, Spokane Garry and one of his brothers accompanied the Governor and his party during the remainder of their stay in the Spokane country.[3]

Lieutenant R. Saxon, speaking of the Spokane Indians, says: "They are noble specimens of the race. Their Chief, Garry, speaks tolerable English. He is rich, powerful and owns a great number of horses."[4]

Mr. George Gibbs, another member of the Stevens party, who paid special attention to gathering statistics and information concerning the Indians, says: "Garry[5] is 42 years old. He is very intelligent, speaks English very fluently and bears an excellent character. He is what he claims to be, and what few are among these tribes, a chief. His lodge in neatness and comfort was far beyond anything we had seen. His family was dressed in the costume of the whites, which, in fact, now prevails over their own. The Chief offered us the hospitality of his house with much cordiality—a cup of tea or coffee and bread."[6]

GARRY'S COUNTRY AND THE INCOMING WHITES

The Spokane nation was composed of three branches or families: the Upper Spokanes occupying the Spokane Valley between the falls and the lands of the Pend Oreilles and Coeur d'Alenes, and to the north and south; the Middle Spokanes occupying the lands about "old Spokane House," Deep Creek and the Four Lakes country; and the Lower Spokanes living about the Tchimokaine, Tumtum (Little Falls), and the mouth of the Spokane River.[7] These spots were their homes, but parties bent on hunting, barter or pleasure roamed about at will from Southern Oregon and Idaho to British Columbia, and from Puget Sound and the ocean to the east slope of the Rocky Mountains, though hunting parties to the "buffalo country" were by no means as frequent as from the Flathead and Kootenai tribes. Generally speaking, the Spokanes claimed as their own all the territory extending from the head waters of the Chimokaine to the mouth of the Spokane River; down the south side of the Columbia as far as the mouth of the Okanogan; south to the head of the Snake River water shed; east to about the line of the present towns of Post Falls and Rathdrum.[8]

They had many horses; their country was well supplied with edible roots and game; while their fisheries on the Spokane, Little Spokane, and Latou (Hangman's) Creek furnished an abundance of salmon, trout, and carp or suckers. These were easily caught in traps and willow baskets, and were so plentiful on most occasions that they were freely furnished to all passersby.[9] The most fertile garden spots in their land were enclosed and cultivated by them.

Spokane Garry was now (1850-60) in his prime, and his tribe, numbering from 500 to 600 people (Middle and Upper Spokane), were prosperous, happy and contented. Though they wandered about and camped at will, they had two principal villages, one at Spokane House; another, on the prairie north of Saltese and Liberty Lakes.

A change now began to take place in the affairs of the Spokane

54

Indians. Settlers began coming in to take possession of their lands. In 1854 the Sinclair party of emigrants arrived overland from Manitoba, some settling on Spokane lands. In 1853 Francis B. Owens, a cattleman, driven out of the St. Mary's Valley in Montana by the Blackfeet Indians, brought some 600 or 700 cattle and 500 horses to feed on the range in the Spokane Valley.[10] The newly discovered Colville mines in the summer of 1855 brought numerous adventurers into the Spokane country, many of whom had little, if any, regard for the rights of the Indians. The proposals made by Governor Stevens at the great Walla Walla Indian Council in 1855 to deprive the Indians of a large part of their lands and to restrict them to reservations began to cause great uneasiness in the minds of all of the Indians in the Columbia River basin. In the summer of 1855 the Cayuses, Yakimas, Walla Wallas, Umatillas, Palouses and many of the tribes in Oregon broke out in war against the whites. According to the Historian Bancroft, Chief Garry, in 1855, reported to the Indian agent, A.J. Bolon, at The Dalles, the murder of the miners by the Yakima Indians near Snoqualmie Pass, and was one of the last persons to talk with that unfortunate officer, who at once started out for the Yakima camp to investigate the matter; returning from the camp Mr. Bolon was murdered by the Yakima Indians.[11]

THE INDIAN COUNCILS AND GARRY AS AN ORATOR

Chief Garry was present at the great Walla Walla Council, but as an observer only, as it was intended to hold a separate council for his tribe and those further north.[12] George Schon [Gustavus Sohon], the artist accompanying Governor Stevens' party, drew a sketch of Garry on May 27, 1855, while Garry was at the council. A reproduction of this sketch, which Garry signed, appears on page thirty-six. [13]

On November 29, 1855, Governor Stevens, hastening back from his treaty with the Blackfeet Indians at Fort Benton on receipt of intelligence of the outbreak of the Columbia River Indians, called a council of the Indians on the Spokane River. Chief Garry met the Governor that day, and on December 3, 4, 5, 1855, a council was held, at which the Spokanes openly sympathized with the hostilities.

Chief Garry, in his opening speech in this council, said to Governor Stevens:

> When I heard of the war I had two hearts, and have had two hearts ever since. The bad heart is a little larger than the good. Now I am thinking if you do not make peace with the Yakimas, war will come into this country like the waters of the sea. From the time of my first recollection, no blood has ever been on the hands of my people. Now that I am grown up I am afraid that we may have the blood of the whites upon our hands.
>
> I hope that you will make peace on the other side of the Columbia and keep the soldiers from coming here. The Americans and the Yakimas are fighting and I think they are both equally guilty.[14] If there were many Frenchmen here, my heart would be like fighting. These French people here have been talking too much. I went to the Walla Walla Council and when I returned I found that all the Frenchmen (settlers in the Colville valley—former employees of the Hudson's Bay Company) had gotten their land written down on a paper. I asked them "Why are you in such a hurry to have writings for your lands now? Why don't you wait until a treaty is made?" Governor, these troubles are on my mind all the time, and I will not hide them. When you first commenced to speak you said the Walla Wallas, Cayuses and Umatillas were to move onto the Nez Perce reservation *and the Spokanes were to move there also. Then I thought you spoke bad. Then I thought you would strike the Indians to the heart.* After you had spoken those nine different things as schools and shops and farms, if you had then asked the chiefs to mark out a piece of land—a pretty large piece to give you—it would not have struck the Indians so to heart. Your thought was good. you see far. But the Indians, being dull-headed, do not see far. Now your children have fallen. The Indians spilled their blood, because they have not sense enough to understand you. Those who killed Pu-pu-mox-mox's son in California, they were Americans. Why are these Americans alive now? Why were they not hanged? That is what the Indians think, that it will be these young people—my people. I do not

56

know their minds, but if they will listen to you I will be very glad. When you talk to your soldiers and tell them not to cross Snake River into our country, I shall be glad.[15]

Later in the same council, Chief Garry spoke again, this time making a strong plea for a "square deal" for his countrymen.

When you look at the red men, you think *you* have more heart, more sense, than these poor Indians. I think that the difference between us and you Americans is in the clothing; the blood and the body are the same. Do you think that because your mother was white and theirs dark, that you are higher or better? We are dark, yet if we cut ourselves the blood is red, so with the whites it is the same, though their skin is white. I do not think we are poor because we belong to another nation. If you take the Indians for men, treat them so now. If you talk to the Indians to make peace, the Indian will do the same to you. You see now the Indians are proud. On account of one of your remarks, some of your people have already fallen to the ground. The Indians are *not* satisfied with the land you gave them. What commenced the trouble was the murder of Pu-pu-mox-mox's son and Dr. Whitman, and now they find their reservation too small. If all those Indians had marked out their own reservations, the trouble would not have happened. If you could get their reservations made a little larger, they would be pleased. If I had the business to do, I could fix it by giving them a little more land. Talking about land I am only speaking my mind. What I was saying yesterday not crossing the soldiers to this side of the Columbia is my business. Those Indians have gone to war and I don't know myself how to fix it up. That is your business. Since, Governor, the beginning of the world there has been war. Why cannot you manage to keep peace? Maybe there will be no peace ever. Even if you should hang all the bad people, war would begin again and would never stop.[16]

THE WAR CLOUDS GATHER

This council, which Governor Stevens declared was one of the stormiest councils that ever occurred in his whole Indian experience, because he would not promise the assembled Indians that the United States troops would not cross to the north of the Snake River, ended in expressions of friendly sentiments, and the

Spokane Indians not only furnished Governor Stevens' party with fresh horses, in place of their jaded steeds, but also gave up some of their own rifles, which Stevens needed to arm his force,[17] and offered to act as his escort as far as the Snake River.[18] The council did not secure for the Indians any substantial concessions from Stevens' plan to place them on small reservations, nor prevent the government troops from crossing the Snake River and invading the Spokane country, and causing the hostile war chiefs, Owhi, Kamiakin and Qualchien, and their warriors to mingle with and incite the northern tribes to fight the whites.

Spokane Garry was all the time uneasy over the situation, as shown by his frequent letters to Governor Stevens. Rumors were being circulated among the peaceful Spokanes, Coeur d'Alene and other northern Indians by the hostile Yakima and Cayuse Indians to the effect that the whites intended to exterminate them. The talk of belligerent Indian agents, volunteer troops and excited newspaper writers formed a substantial basis for these reports.

On February 10, 1856, Special Agent B.F. Shaw, at Vancouver, Washington, in his report to Governor Stevens on the situation of the Indian affairs, said: ''The Spokanes and the Coeur d'Alenes will remain friendly in case an agent can be with them all the time to give them the correct news; but unless this is done the hostiles will circulate all kinds of reports among them which will be believed unless contradicted.''[19]

At the Indian council called by Kamiaken at the Camas grounds south of the Spokane in May, 1858, the brothers of Kamiacken told the assembled Indians: ''Friends in Col. Wright's command have told us that the whites intend to wage an indiscriminate war against all the Indians in the whole country; that the whites only wished to keep them separate so that it would be easier to kill them all; that it was a certain fact they all had to die, and they had better take up their guns and all go to war together.''[20]

During this time the following letters passed between Spokane Garry and Governor Stevens:

THE CASE OF SPOKANE GARRY

Spokane River, September 12, 1856

Sir: You had desired our going to meet you at the treaty, but we cannot go on account of the salmon, which is coming up now, and we are laying in our winter's supply; as that is our only resource for living, we think we cannot do without it. As for us, we are for peace; and it does not make any difference about our not going to meet you, for we all want to remain quiet and peaceful. The Coeur d'Alenes have all left, but one chief, for the buffalo country, and my people are going also as soon as salmon is over. I have heard that the Nez Perces were talking of war. That makes me uneasy, and study much; for my part I don't like to see them take up their arms, for they will gain nothing by it. I have heard that you talk hard about us, by Indians, but I don't believe it; but I think it is all the Yakimas' doing, to get us to join them, but I don't believe it, for they want me to go to war by all means; but I would rather be quiet. But I expect you have more confidence in me than that, and hope you will not believe any of their stories, for I know that you know too much to give credit to such idle talk. When we meet next we can have a good understanding together, for I will keep nothing from you and expect the same from you.

So I remain, very respectfully yours,   GARRY.
His Excellency Governor I.I. Stevens.

OFFICE SUPERINTENDENT INDIAN AFFAIRS

Olympia, W.T., October 22, 1856.

I have received your letter of September 12; I don't believe the stories against Garry; I am glad you don't believe the stories against me. The Spokanes have always been good Indians. They did not join Kam-ai-ak-um in the summer; I trust they will not join him now; I am the friend of the Indians. They must not believe the stories of Kam-ai-ak-um and his people. They are like bad children that have done a mean thing that they are ashamed of. They want all the Indians to do the same thing, so that they will be no better than they are. Remember me to Polatkin and the other chiefs. Write to me often.

Your friend,   ISSAC I. STEVENS,
Governor and Superintendent, &c.

Spokane Garry,
    Head Chief of the Spokanes.[21]

In a letter to the Secretary of War, dated February 19, 1856, Governor Stevens stated that the Spokanes had informed him that, "If the Indians now at war were driven into their country they could not answer for the consequences; probably many of the Spokanes would join them."[22]

In his annual report as Superintendent of Indian Affairs for Washington Territory, under the date of November 1, 1856, Governor Stevens stated, with reference to copies of Garry's letters annexed to the report: "It will not be out of place here to state that I have written and received letters the past season from all the chiefs of the Spokanes and neighboring tribes, and in the case of Garry several letters have been received. Many of these letters are significant of the state of feeling there and I would send copies of them if they could be prepared by this mail, but being generally in French I have found time to translate but a few of them."[23]

In a letter to Major General John Wool, commanding the Department of the Pacific, dated March 20, 1856, Governor Stevens wrote as follows:

> I have recently heard from the Nez Perces, the Coeur d'Alenes and the Spokanes. The former are firm in their allegiance. But the Spokanes urge me to have a military force in the great prairie between them and the hostile Indians, so that these latter may not be driven into their country, and thus incite the young men to war.
>
> The letter of Garry, Chief of the Spokanes, is a most plaintive and earnest call for help, so his hands may be strengthened in keeping his people to their plighted faith; and the coincidence is remarkable, that this Indian chief, a white man in education and views of life, should ask me to do the very thing I have urged upon you; for you will remember, in my memoir, I urge that the troops in operating against the Indians, should be interposed between the friendly and hostile tribes, to prevent those now friendly from joining in the war. I have, sir, studied the character of these Indians, and my views as to the influence upon the friendly Indians, of the mode of carrying on the war against the hostiles, are confirmed by the only highly

educated Indian of either Oregon or Washington, and the head chief of the very tribe in reference to which I have made this recommendation and felt the most solicitude."[24]

The acts of the volunteer troops in murdering Chief Pu-Pu-Mox-Mox while a prisoner of war, the slaughter of numerous Indian non-combatants, including women and children, the taking of cattle and supplies from friendly Indians, and the plundering of their caches all lent color and intent to the spoken threat to exterminate the Indians.[25]

The intent and purpose of Colonel Steptoe in bringing his forces north of the Snake River was not understood by the northern Indians. It was persistently rumored that the government intended to seize the lands of the Indians, and the agitation of the Yakima braves greatly excited the Indians, many of whom felt justly incensed at what they thought was an armed invasion of their country by an armed force bent on conquest.

FOUR OF SPOKANE GARRY'S BOOKS LOANED TO RICHARD LEWIS AND JEROME PELTIER BY MRS. JOSIE PARR AND MRS. CHRISTINE ELLENWOOD OF WORLEY, IDAHO. COURTESY OF RICHARD T. LEWIS.

FOOTNOTES ON CHAPTER II

1   Pacific Ry. Reports, Vol. 12, pp. 136, 148.

2   Pacific Ry. Reports, Vol. 12, p. 148.

3   Pacific Ry. Reports, Vol. 12, p. 149; *Life Gen. I.I. Stevens*, Vol. 1, p. 399.

4   Pacific Ry. Reports, Vol. 1, p. 256.

5   The Indians pronounced the name as if it was spelled "Jerry"—Curtis, *North American Indian*, Vol. VII, p. 55.

6   Pacific Ry. Reports, Vol. 1, pp. 414-415.

7   George Gibbs, writing in 1853, states that the Spokanes are composed of eight bands:
     1. The Sin-slik-hoo-ish, on the plains above the Coeur d'Alene crossing.
     2. The Sin-too-too-ish, on the river above the forks.
     3. The Sma-hoo-men-a-ish, at the forks.
     4. The Skai-schil-t'nish, at the old Chimokaine Mission.
     5. The Ski-chei-a-mouse, above the Colville trail.
     6. The Schu-el-stitsh, on the Columbia.
     7. The Sin-poil-shue, on the Columbia.
     8. The Sin-spee-ish, on the Columbia.
   The latter three bands are a distinct branch of the Seelish (*sic*) Nation. Curtis (Vol. 7, p. 54) does not recognize either the first or the fifth bands and confines the Spokanes to the Sin-tu-tu-li, or Muddy Creek people (Upper Spokanes); the Sin-ho-mene, or Salmon Trout people (Middle Spokanes); and the Tsk-ais-tsih-lin, the people about the Little Falls (Lower Spokanes): the three being identical with bands 2, 3 and 4 named by Gibbs. Garry's band, the Middle Spokanes, usually resided in early days at the forks of the Spokane (1 Pac. Ry. Report, p. 414); later upon his becoming also the leader of the Upper Spokanes he spent most of his time among the Upper Spokanes in the vicinity of the present City of Spokane.

8   See Pacific Ry. Reports, Vol. 1, p. 414, and statement of Nellie Garry.

9   Report Captain John Mullen on construction military road, p. 111.

10   Pacific Ry. Reports, Vol. 1, p. 257; statement John V. Campbell, VII Washington Historical Quarterly, p. 194.

11   Bancroft's *History of Washington, Idaho and Montana*, p. 109.

12   *Life of General I.I. Stevens*, Vol. 2, p. 39.

13   *Life of General I.I. Stevens*, Vol. 2, p. 141.

14   Here Garry is talking about trouble that Louis Brown was causing in the Colville Valley. Louis Brown had to leave the Colville area because of the trouble he caused there. He moved to Montana and later became the founding father of

Frenchtown, Montana. Although the above person seems the most likely individual that Garry was referring to, he may have been thinking about Antoine Plante because the latter person's home was burned to the ground by unknown parties about this time. *Antoine Plante* by Jerome Peltier, pp. 21. Washington Historical Quarterly, July 1916, pages 193, 194.

15   *Life Isaac I. Stevens*, Vol. 2, pp. 136-137.

16   *Life Isaac I. Stevens*, Vol. 2, pp. 139-140; Bancroft's *History of Washington, Idaho and Montana*, p. 105.

17   While at Antoine Plante's on the Spokane River, Governor Stevens organized a military company and named it Stevens' Guards. Not to be outdone miners and others there for the meeting organized another group and named them the Spokane Invincibles.

18   *Life of Isaac I. Stevens*, pp. 134, 139, 141.

19   Serial No. 889, 34th Cong., Ex. D. 37, p. 34.

20   Report of Sub-Indian Agent William Craig, Serial No. 899, 34th Cong., 3rd S. Ex. D. 37, p. 118.

21   Serial No. 899, 34th Cong., 3rd S. Ex. D., pp. 67, 68.

22   Serial No. 822, 34th Cong., 1st Ex. D. 66, p. 5.

23   Serial No. 899, 34th Cong., 3rd S. Ex. D. 37, p. 38.

24   Serial No. 822, 34th Cong., 1st S. Ex. D. 66, p. 43.

25   Serial No. 822, 34th Cong., 1st S. Ex. D. 66, pp. 37, 38, 51.

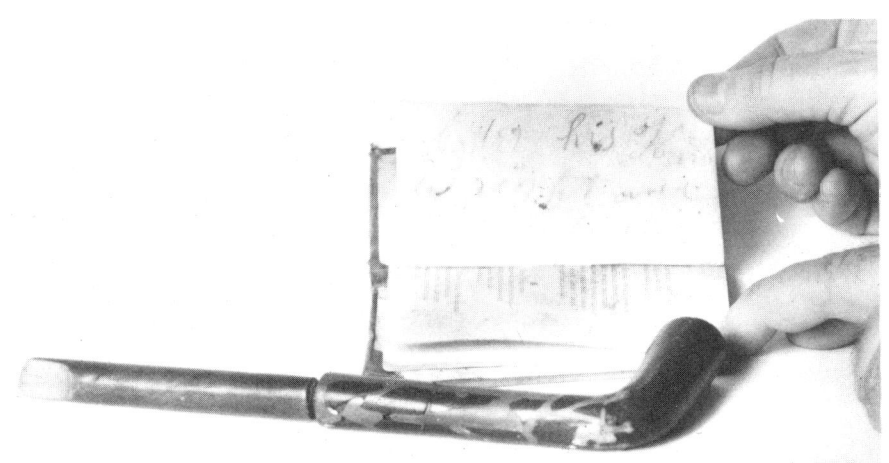

Jerome Peltier's hands holding the flyleaf of Chief Spokane Garry's hymnal. Garry's pipe is in the foreground. Courtesy of Richard T. Lewis.

SITE OF COL. WRIGHT'S CAMP AND OF THE COUNCIL WITH THE SPOKANE INDIANS AT SMITH'S FORD ON HANGMAN CREEK, SEPTEMBER 23, 1858. The MEN IN the picture (left to right) are John E. Smith and Thomas Buell, surviving members of Col. Wright's command. Mr. Smith is pointing out the location of Col. Wright's tent. In the background, beyond the bridge, are the stumps of the trees from which the Indians were hung. (Photograph by Palmer, Spokane, 1916.)

64

CHAPTER III

GARRY AND THE SPOKANE CHIEFS TRIED TO PREVENT THE ATTACK ON STEPTOE'S COMMAND

The vicinity of Rosalia and Spring Valley had from time immemorial been the favorite gathering ground of the Indians, who annually visited the locality with their families to secure their camas and other roots which grew there in profusion.

On the approach of the soldiers, Garry and some of the other chiefs rode into Colonel Steptoe's camp and had a talk with him, asking that he explain to the Indians the nature of his expedition, and stating to him the resentment of the Indians and the grave danger of conflict should he continue. After the interview with Colonel Steptoe, Spokane Garry returned to his people and told them and the other Indians that the soldiers did not want to attack the Indians and were merely traveling through their country.[1] Up to this time it was the proud boast of the Spokane, Coeur d'Alene and Pend Oreille Indians, all off-shoots of the great Saleesh(*sic*) nation, that in fifty years' intercourse with the whites none from their respective tribes had ever shed the blood of a white man. That this record was broken in 1858 was due, in a large measure, to the white man's failure to understand the Indians and to deal fairly and considerately with them in the matter of reservations.[2]

THE ATTACK ON STEPTOE'S COMMAND

Colonel Steptoe, in his official report to Major W.W. Mackall, written at Walla Walla on May 23, 1858, states: "Toward night, a party of chiefs rode up to talk with me. * * * *" During the conference the Indians refused to furnish him with canoes with which to cross the Spokane River. Continuing, Colonel Steptoe says: "I concluded for this reason to retrace my steps at once and the next morning turned back towards this post.[3]

Ten or twelve hundred young Indian bucks from the various tribes, decked out in war paint and eager for a fight, had gathered. Owhi, Qualchein, Kamiaken, and other warriors from the Yakimas and Cayuses, were urging them on to fight, and Garry, with the other head men, were having a great deal of trouble in keeping them quiet. It was even intimated that some of the Nez Perce scouts with Steptoe urged the hostile Indians to attack his command. On May 17, 1858, near the present town of Rosalia, the warriors of the Yakimas, Palouses, Coeur d'Alenes and other tribes attacked and defeated Colonel Steptoe's command, and forced it to beat a retreat back across the Snake River. After the attack had been commenced, many of the young men of the Spokanes joined in the hostilities. A considerable quantity of booty in the way of horses, mules, guns, blankets and camp equipment was secured by the Indians.

It is a well settled fact that Spokane Garry and the other Spokane chiefs under him used every effort to restrain their young men. One of these young Indian fighters, in telling of the Steptoe battle, has stated: "All the time the head men were trying to hold back the young men. * * * * The Spokane chiefs succeeded for a time in holding us. Before long, however, all of us were engaged in the fighting."[4]

GARRY'S EFFORTS TO PREVENT FURTHER CONFLICT

After the defeat and retreat of Colonel Steptoe's force in May, 1858, a threat was made by the Government that, unless the leaders of the attack on Colonel Steptoe were surrendered by the various tribes, indiscriminate punishment would be meted out to them. Chief Garry, learning of the intention of the Government to send Colonel Wright north of the Snake River in charge of a strong punative expedition, and desiring to avoid a second conflict of arms between the Indians and the white soldiers, joined with several of the leading chiefs in sending personal letters to General Clark, commander of the Department of the Columbia, in August, 1858, in an effort to persuade the Government not to bring further troops into the Spokane country to punish or attack the Indians. Upon the subject of surrendering their relatives to General Clark for punishment the chiefs were in unison, Chief Soulotkin (Polatkin) wrote: "You can kill me, but I will not deliver my neighbor." Chief Melkaposi wrote: "I am unwilling to give you up my three brothers. * * * * As long as I live I don't want you to take possession of my country."

CHIEF GARRY'S MASTERLY PLEA FOR PEACE

Spokane Garry reviewed at length the misunderstanding between the whites and the Indians, pointing out the mistake which had been made in not consulting the Indians as to the size and location of their proposed reservation, and the injustice of seeking to punish Indians for violations of the white man's laws, without having first made such laws known to the Indians. His letter is as follows:[5]

> You, General Clark, you are my friend. I am very much sorry for the battle which took place. I think that you have fought for nothing. The blood of your soldiers and the Indians has been spilled. If there should have been a just cause of fighting, I would not regret it; though there should be killed on both sides, I would not then be much sorry for it.
>
> Now, I am at a loss what to think of it, for you say, you white people, this is my country; you American and English, claim the land, and the Indians, each on his side of the line you have drawn.[6] Then you make a useless war with Indians; you cause trouble to the whites living hereabout, and you have nothing to gain from the war.
>
> Now I hear that somebody—you perhaps, General Clark—want to make peace. I would be very glad no enmity should be left. I, Indian, am unacquainted with your ways, as you with mine. When you meet me, you Americans, you are ignorant of the uses of the Indians. When you meet me, we talk friendly; we shake hands.
>
> Two years after you met me, you American, I heard words from

white people, whence I concluded you wanted to kill me for my land. I did not believe it. Every year I have heard the same.

Now you arrived; you my friend; you Stevens, in Whiteman (*sic*) Valley (W.W.); you called the Indians to that place. I went there to listen to what should be said. You had a speech you, my friend Stevens, to the Indians. You spoke for the land of the Indian. You told them all what you should pay them for their land.

I was much pleased when I heard how much you offered: Annual money, houses, schools, blacksmiths, farms, etc. And then you said, all the Cayuses, Walla Walla and Spokanes should emigrate to Layers (Lawyer's) country; and from Colville and below all Indians should go and stay to Camayaken's (*sic*) country; and by saying so you broke the hearts of all the Indians; and, hearing that, I thought that you missed it.

Should you have given the Indians time to think on it, and to tell you what portion of their land they wanted to give, it would have been right. Then the Indians got mad and began to kill you whites. I was very sorry all the time.

Then you began to war against the Indians.

When you began this war all the upper country was very quiet. Then every year we heard something from the lower Indians. I told the people hereabouts not to listen to such talk. The governor will come up, you will hear from his own mouth; then believe it.

Now this spring I heard of the coming of Colonel Steptoe. I did my best to persuade my people not to shoot him. He goes to Colville, I said, to speak to the whites and to the Indians. We will go there and listen to what he shall say.

They would not listen to me, but the boys shot at him; I was very sorry. When the fight was over, I was thinking all the time to make peace, until I was told that Colonel Steptoe had said "I won't make peace now with the Coeur d'Alenes and Spokanes. I will first shoot them (he said) and then, when they shall be very sorry, I will grant them peace." Hearing that, I thought it was useless for me to try to make peace; and when I hear now what you say, what you write here to the Indians, there is one word which you won't do.

Until now you never came to an understanding with the Indians to let them know your laws. You ask some to be delivered up. Poor Indians can't come to that. But this one word, and sure you will make peace. Then calling a meeting of the chiefs, you will let them know your law, and the law being known, all those who shall continue to misbehave, red and white, may be hung. The Indians will have no objection to that.

I am very sorry the war has begun. Like the fire in a dry prairie, it will spread all over the country, until now so peaceful. I hear already from different parts rumors of other Indians ready to take in. Make peace, and then American soldiers may go about; we won't care. That's my own private opinion.

Peace being made, it won't be difficult to come to a good understanding with these Indians. You, General Clarke, if you think proper to withdraw the sword, peace will be easy.

Please answer us, for we want it.

GARRY

CHIEF GARRY'S PEACE PLEA IGNORED

On August 18, 1858, General Clark, writing from headquarters of the Department of the Pacific at Fort Vancouver, in a letter to Fathers M. Congiato and J. Joset of the Coeur d'Alene mission, refused to recede from his arbitrary demand that the Spokane Indians surrender such of their friends and relatives as were leading participants in the attack on Steptoe. In this insistence General Clark, as had many Government officials and army officers, wholly failed to understand some traits of Indian character—their pride, independence, and tribal and family loyalty. A close observer of Western Indian life, himself a son of an Indian mother, has said, concerning the Northwest tribes in their native environment, that they have "an independence of spirit which neither force nor kindness can subdue; not that they are unsusceptible to kindness or amenity from the whites, but that they will bend to no man, and are exceedingly lordly to all comers."[7]

Throughout Spokane Garry's correspondence at that time, there is a patient, insistent demand that the Indians, themselves, be consulted as to the disposition of their land and the location of their proposed reservations. The letters of Chiefs Garry, Polatkin and Melkaposi to General Clark failed in their purpose, and the army officers, especially Colonel Wright, seemed to have taken offense at the independent tone of the writers.[8]

A few days later the troops left Fort Walla Walla, and on August 27, 1858, started north from the Snake River for the Spokane country.

HOSTILITIES NEAR SPOKANE

On September 1, 1858, this punitive expedition under Colonel Wright came in contact with the allied Yakimas, Spokanes, Palouses, Coeur d'Alenes and Pend Oreille Indians in the Four Lakes country, in the vicinity of the present town of Meadow Lake. the Indians put up a brave fight, but the soldiers, by reason of their superior arms, defeated the Indians without the loss of a single man either killed or wounded; while wounding forty or fifty Indians and killing fifteen or twenty. Among the latter were a brother and brother-in-law of Chief Garry.[9] On the 5th of September, on the Spokane plains a few miles southwest from Spokane House, Colonel Wright again came in contact with the Indian forces, and in a running fight for a distance of fourteen miles again inflicted a disastrous defeat on the allied Indians; but one soldier was wounded in the fight, while many Indians were killed, including two Spokane chiefs and two brothers of Chief Garry.[10]

GARRY DID NOT FIGHT THE WHITES

While it has been frequently stated that Chief Garry took part in the Indian war, it seems to be established clearly that he held aloof from the fighting.[11] Dr. Perkins mentions that at the Indian council of the Spokanes at Fort Colville, though Garry never said a word, but merely looked on, he expressed himself to the doctor in these words: "My heart is undecided, I do not know which way to go. My friends are fighting the whites. I do not like to join them, but if I do not they will kill me."[12] All of Garry's brothers and relatives took an active part in the fighting, and Garry himself sympathized with them in their protest against Stevens' proposal to take away their lands, without their consent, and to herd them like cattle onto small reservations, arbitrarily selected by the whites, and against the invasion of their country by the white soldiers; but his long and peaceful association with the white men made him unwilling to take up arms against them. Besides, Garry saw, as an educated Indian familiar with the civilization east of the mountains, the futility of resisting the whites. He made earnest efforts to restrain the Spokanes from fighting, but his efforts were futile.

Garry himself told the old settlers that he took no part in the fighting; this is also confirmed by the statements of Curley Jim and of Garry's daughter, Nellie. The latter states that they were threshing their grain at the time of the big fight and that Chief Garry had gone to Colville to get some supplies. While he was gone the Indians went to battle with the soldiers. "We sent word to Chief Garry and he returned. * * * * Chief Garry stopped his people, but the Coeur d'Alene Indians wanted to fight more."[13]

On September 6th Colonel Wright moved his troops up on the south side of the Spokane River. While on the march, some Indians came down on the north side of the Spokane River and, calling across, stated that Chief Garry was near and wanted to talk with Colonel Wright, and the Colonel told them to have Garry meet him at the ford two miles above the falls. Soon after the soldiers reached their camp on the south bank of the river, in what is now Dennis and Bradley's Addition. Garry crossed at the ford which was near the present Mission Avenue bridge,[14] and held a conference with Wright. Chief Garry told Wright that he was opposed to the fighting, but that the young men and many of the chiefs were against him, and that he could not control his people. Bancroft states that in view of his conduct and his well-known previous character there was no reason to doubt Garry's assertion. Lieutenant Kip expresses the same view.[15] Notwithstanding this, Colonel Wright treated Garry coldly and curtly told him to tell his people and all other Indians to come in at once with their women and children, and lay down their arms, or he would fight them until they were exterminated.[16] Colonel Wright directed Chief Garry and Big Star to call a council of the leading Indians to meet him on his return from the Coeur d'Alene country, and make a peace treaty with him.

TRAGIC EVENTS NEAR SPOKANE

The next day Wright's command moved up the river about fifteen miles and camped; here a companion of Polotkin, one of the Spokane Chiefs who had come to Wright's camp above the Big Falls and surrendered, was hanged. On the 8th, at Liberty Lake, near the winter camping grounds of the Spokanes, Colonel Wright captured between 800 and 900 Indian horses,[17] together with considerable supplies and equipment.[18] On September 10th these horses were slaughtered at Wright's order as a punishment to the Indians. The site of the slaughter of these horses by the soldiers was on the bank of the Spokane River, a little above Colonel Wright's camp, a spot until recent years marked by a scattered pile of bones in the open prairie, and was appropriately called "Horse Slaughter Camp." In the vicinity a number of Indian houses, filled with grain, were found. These were burned. Chief Garry used to tell the pioneers that he had witnessed the killing of these horses from the foothills; in the telling, as with many tales oft repeated, the number had grown to between 2000 and 3000.[19] Chief Garry also told Major Gwydir, a former Indian agent, and such other pioneers as he would talk to, that he never wanted his folks (the Spokanes) to fight, and that he did all that he could to stop the war.[20]

THE TREATY WITH THE SPOKANES

Returning from his treaty with the Coeur d'Alene Indians at the DeSmet Mission on September 23, 1858, Colonel Wright camped on Latah Creek, about twenty miles above its mouth, and held a council with representatives of the Spokane, Colville, Pend Oreille and other small bands, who had been gathered together by Chiefs Garry and Big Star. One hundred and seven Indian delegates attended, and the peace treaty was signed by all the chiefs present for the Spokanes. The council was held at what is known as Smith's Ford, on Latah Creek.[21] The Spokane Chiefs, Garry and Big Star, signed the treaty, but were absent during a part of the council in an effort to bring into camp the Yakima Chief Kamiaken.[22] They returned and reported to Colonel

72

Wright that Kamiaken could not be persuaded to come into Wright's camp. Subsequent acts of Colonel Wright proved that Kamiaken was justified in his caution.

HOW HANGMAN CREEK GOT ITS NAME

On the morning of September 24, 1858, Qualchien, the Yakima Chief, came boldly into Wright's camp. He was at once seized by Wright's command, and the Colonel made the following laconic report: "Qualchien came to camp at nine this morning and at nine-fifteen he was hanged."[23]

Three days later, his father, Chief Owhi, was shot by Wright's soldiers while attempting to escape from the guard near Snake River crossing.[24] Eight more Indians were hung in the Spokane country by Wright's orders, four more on the Palouse, and four more at Walla Walla. Chief Garry was probably a silent and disapproving spectator at several of these summary executions of the Indians. Local Indians and pioneers used to point out in the early '80s a pine tree as the place where several of these Indians were hung by Colonel Wright's order.[25] So far as known, no Spokane Indians were executed by Colonel Wright. The Indian hung at "Horse Slaughter Camp" was a Palouse; those hung on Hangman Creek, on the Palouse and at Walla Walla were all from the Yakima, Walla Walla and Cayuse tribes.

FOOTNOTES ON CHAPTER III

1   Statement of Thomas Garry. *et al.*

2   "In the majority of cases, Indian wars are to be traced to the aggressions of lawless white men." Report Special Joint Committee on Indian Affairs, U.S. Senate January 26, 1867, p. 5. In nearly every instance difficulties between Indians and the whites arose from aggression on the Indians by the Whites.—Colonel Bent, appendix ditto, p. 93. As a general thing, the difficulties (with Indians) arose from aggressions on the part of the whites.—Colonel Kit Carson, appendix ditto, p. 96.

   The whites began the Seminole war. General Sherman used to say that they began every war. * * * * Surely our action, legislative and executive, was usually hostile—never really friendly." —General Howard's *Life and Experiences*, pp. 368-9

3   See Colonel Steptoe's report, Manring's *Conquest of the Coeur d'Alenes*, pp. 84, 86, 90, 128, 136, H. Ex. Doc. No. 2, p. 346, 35th Congress, 2nd Sess., and Curtis' *North American Indian*, Vol. 7, p. 59.

4   Curtis' *North American Indian*, Vol. VII, p. 59. In a letter to Father Congiato, dated June 27, 1858, Father Joset of the Coeur d'Alene Mission wrote: "Vincent (a Coeur d'Alene Chief) and the Spokane Chief (Garry) prevented the fight on the 15th inst." —Manring's *Conquest of the Coeur d'Alenes*, etc., pp. 148-9. See also statement Thomas Garry, *et al.*, *supra*. In a letter to General Clark, dated August 3, 1858, Father Congiato wrote: "I have had a long conversation with Spokane Garry. He is strongly for peace." H. Ex. Doc. No. 2, *supra*, p. 374.

5   Manring's *Conquest of the Coeur d'Alenes*, pp. 162-6. House Ex. Doc. No. 2, *supra*, pp. 376-7.

6   Garry refers to the line between Canada and the United States on the 49th parallel. Commenting on the same subject at Colville, Garry has said: "One man with the party came from the cold side of Heaven and says this is my country; up to this line all the country is mine. The man with his party from the warm side of Heaven says the land on this side is mine; and so they settled it; and we, the poor Indians, have nothing to say about it." —Serial No. 974, 35th Cong., S.H.E. No. 95, p. 619.

7   Ranald MacDonald Mms., p. 64, in the Library of the Spokane Historical Society.

8   Bancroft's *History of the Pacific Northwest, Oregon and Washington*. Vol. 1, p. 636, Manring's *Conquest of the Coeur d'Alenes, Spokanes, etc.*, pp. 161-166.

9   Kip's *Army Life on the Pacific*, pp. 59, 133, 142. H. Ex. Doc. No. 2, *supra*, pp. 386-390.

10 Kip's *Army Life on the Pacific*, pp. 63, 138, 143. H. Ex. Doc. 2, *supra*, pp. 390-393. These army reports are incorrect. No brothers of Garry were killed in the fighting, but two cousins were killed. Hung p'ong l'glee and Tsch-loustsch. Statement Thomas Garry, *et al.*

11 See statements of Nellie Garry and Curley Jim, *supra*.

12 Kip's *Army Life on the Pacific*, p. 67. In a letter dated on the Spokane River, July 16, 1858, John Owen, Special Indian Agent, wrote: "I fear Spokane Garry, he will be forced, in my opinion, to make common cause with the enemy," though in a previous letter from Colville dated July 11, 1858, he states that Spokane Garry and Skoll-Holl had given him friendly advice as to the disposition of the hostile Indians. Serial No. 997, Doc. No. 95, p. 618, Serial No. 997-995-621.

13 Statements Nellie Garry and Curley Jim, *supra*.

14 Kip's *Army Life on the Pacific*, p. 67. See Wright's report, Serial No. 984, 35th Cong., 2nd Session, S.E. Doc. No. 15, p. 25.

15 Bancroft's *History of Washington, Idaho and Montana*, p. 190; Kip's *Army Life on the Pacific*, p. 67. See also Victor's *Indian Wars of Oregon*, p. 496.

16 Kip's *Army Life on the Pacific*, p. 67.

17 "Tragic Events Near Spokane" tells the story of 800 to 900 Indian horses being captured. It is generally accepted that there were 1000 in the herd of which 800 were slain and two hundred were retained for use by the troops.

18 Kip's *Army Life on the Pacific*, p. 67. Wright's report, Serial No. 984, 35th Congress, 2nd Session, S.E. Doc. No. 15, p. 26.

19 Gen. M.R. Morgan gives the number of horses at 1,400 in his reminiscences under date July 19, 1907.

20 Statement of Major Gwydir, Library Spokane Historical Society, Kip, pp. 70, 71.

21 Serial No. 1051, 36th Cong., 1st S. Ex. Doc. 65, pp. 90-1. Manring's *Conquest of the Coeur d'Alenes*, pp. 226-9. A copy of the treaty is set out in the Appendix "A" hereto.

22 Kip's *Army Life on the Pacific*, p. 91. Manring's *Conquest of the Coeur d'Alenes*, etc. pp. 228-232.

23 This summary execution by Colonel Wright without charges or trial was contrary to the Anglo-Saxon spirit of justice and fair play and wholly unjustified. In instructing Spokane Garry to call in the Indians, Colonel Wright had said: "Say that if they do as I demand *no life should be taken*." The killing of Qualchien was in direct violation of Wright's previous pledge of amnesty. (Report of Colonel Wright, Serial No. 984, Doc. No. 15, p. 225.)

24 Kip's *Army Life on the Pacific*, pp. 104-106.

25 In the hanging of these Indians, Mr. Thomas Beall, now of Lewiston, Idaho, was detailed to act as hangman. He has personally identified, on a recent visit, the site of these executions on Hangman's Creek to be at "Smith's Ford." The stumps of the tree are still in existance and iron gas pipes containing Mr. Beall's statements have been buried under these stumps for identification.

THE LAST OF THE SPOKANES
Trespassers on lands which their forefathers held for
untold ages. Photograph by Palmer, Spokane, 1916.

CHAPTER IV

GARRY'S REQUEST FOR A RESERVATION

n the early spring of 1859, Chief Garry, on behalf of his people, presented the following petition to military authorities and the Indian agent:

Walla Walla, W.T., March 28, 1859

Sir: My people are desirous of having peace with the whites. Their wish is to have an Indian agent and soldiers to live in their country to protect them. All the chiefs and all the people are ready and willing to make a treaty with the government for the sale of their lands. They are perfectly satisfied with having roads made through their country.

For myself, if a "treaty" is made with us for our lands, I wish our reservation to be located where we will not be interrupted by the whites, nor our people have a chance to interrupt the whites. We have so many dishonest men who would steal from the whites, if they were near them that it would occasion us much trouble.

My horses have given out, and it is so late in the spring I will have to return home to attend to my crops, or I would go and see you. If you should visit here this spring the Indian agent will send me word, and I will come down and see you.

I have the honor to be, very respectfully, your most obedient servant,

SPOKANE GARRY.

Witness, A.J. Cain,
    Indian Agent, Washington Territory.
Brig. Gen. W.S. Harney,
    Commanding Department of Oregon and Washington,
        Fort Vancouver, W.T.''[1]

This letter was forwarded to the Adjutant General with the following communication:

Headquarters Department of Oregon,
Fort Vancouver, W.T., April 7, 1859.

Sir: I have the honor to enclose a copy of a communication from "Spokan Garry," one of the principal chiefs of the Spokan Indians, in which he states his people are desirous to be placed upon a reservation where they will neither disturb nor be disturbed by the whites.

In justice to these Indians this step should be adopted by our government; they already cultivate the soil in part for subsistence, and unless protected in their right to do so, they will be forced into a miserable warfare until they are exterminated.

I have received repeated assurance during the past winter from these and other Indians of this department of their earnest and sincere desires to maintain peace with the whites, and be content with whatever measures the government may effect in relation to their country.

I am, sir, very respectfully, your obedient servant,
W.S. HARNEY,
Brigadier General, Commanding.

Assistant Adjutant General,
Headquarters of the Army, New York City.

These communications were duly called to the attention of the Secretary of the Interior,[2] but no action ever seems to have been taken on them.

GARRY'S EFFORTS TO PRESERVE PART OF HIS COUNTRY AS A RESERVATION AND LATER INDIAN COUNCILS AND CONFERENCES

In the spring of 1859, Spokane Garry, with other principal chiefs of the mountain tribes, accompanied Father DeSmet to Forts Walla Walla and Vancouver for a conference with the general in command of the Department of Columbia, and the Superintendent of Indian Affairs. Father DeSmet met Garry in the Spokane Prairie and, representing to him that poor old Kamiakin had no horse suitable to take him on such a long journey, Chief Garry sent Kamiakin a horse and an invitation to join the other chiefs and accompany them on the trip.[3]

On the arrival of the party at Fort Vancouver, a conference was held on Indian affairs, after which Spokane Garry and the other chiefs spent several weeks visiting the principal towns and cities of Oregon and Washington Territory as guests of the Government.[4]

1874

In June, 1874, General Jefferson C. Davis, Commandant of the Department of the Columbia, at Vancouver held a conference with Chief Garry at the falls of the Spokane. Rev. H.T. Cowley, who had arrived a few days before, and who was present at the interview at Garry's request, states that General Davis gave Garry a very cold shoulder; that he stated that he had no interest in giving a reservation for the Spokane Indians, and brusquely told Garry to be careful not to make any trouble.[5]

1877

On August 16, 1877, another council with the Indians was held at Spokane by General (the Colonel) Frank Wheaton. This was during the time of the Nez Perce war. In July, Chief Joseph had sent a squad of Nez Perce Indians to the Spokanes. They camped in a little grove, just south of the present line of the Northern Pacific tracks, near what is now Washington Street, and held war dances daily in an effort to work upon the Spokanes to join the Nez Perces. Spokane Garry and the other head men were not responsive to their appeals, and requested the Nez Perce envoys to move on; this they did.

At the council subsequently held, the Government representatives promised Chief Garry and the other Spokanes that if they remained at peace they would be well taken care of—a promise as yet unfulfilled.

1880

COLONEL WATKIN'S EMPTY PROMISE

In the summer of 1880, General Howard, with his aide, Captain Wilkinson, and Colonel E.C. Watkins, the Indian Inspector, met the Colville, Upper Spokane, Okanogan, Coeur d'Alene and Lower Spokane Indians in a council held above the falls of the Spokane, at what is now known as Dennis and Bradley's Addition. There were between 3000 and 4000 Indians represented at these councils. Most of these Indians were as yet unprovided for as to reservations. At these councils the Spokanes grouped themselves, some under Chief Moses, others under Chief Garry.

General Howard says: "Garry's main desire was to have a reservation set apart for himself and his followers."[6] The General adds that during the councils Garry showed himself more of a lawyer than a warrior, and at one of the councils made the longest speech of any Indian he ever heard, and that he knew how to filibuster like a Congressman when he had a point to gain by continuous talking. These councils resulted in Colonel Watkins promising a new and ample reservation to the Spokanes and the "renegades" off from the reservations, with metes and bounds well defined. The promise was never fulfilled and the Middle and Upper Spokanes were never given any reservation of their own.

1881

In 1881, General O.O. Howard and Governor Ferry met the Spokane Indians in a council on the prairie now known as Dennis and Bradley's Addition, and announced to the assembled Spokanes that they must take up land in severalty or be placed on a reservation west of the Columbia. The Spokanes were indignant, and Garry, who could speak English very well, voiced their protest thus: "What right have you to dictate to us? This is our country and we will not leave it." This protest was heeded, as the Government did not care to repeat the blunder made in 1877 with the Nez Perces.[7]

1887

The Upper and Middle Spokanes continued to live at such of their old camping grounds as had not been taken possession of by the whites until 1887. In a last Indian council, held in March, 1887, at a livery stable on Riverside Avenue in the town of Spokane Falls, about where the present United States Post Office building is now located, Chief Garry asked the Inspector of the Indian Department and the

Commissioners that his people (the Upper and Middle Spokanes) have ceded to them as a reservation the land on both sides of the Spokane River from the city of Spokane to Tum Tum.[8] The request was not granted.

LAND IN SEVERALTY VS. LAND IN COMMON

Garry's chief ambition and effort in his later years was to secure a treaty with the Government which would preserve a substantial part of his country to his tribe and provide a substantial annuity to them in consideration of their relinquishment of their title to the remaining lands. Garry maintained to the last that such provisions had been promised him by Governor I.I. Stevens in the early '50's and again in the '70's at the council held by the Commissioner of Indian Affairs, when the boundaries of such a reservation were definitely settled and agreed upon.

Strenuous efforts were made by the Government to induce the Spokanes to abandon their title to the lands in the Spokane country and take up lands in severalty under the Indian homestead act. In view of the fact that the Indians of his tribe were accustomed to travel about and to occupy different parts of their country at different seasons of the year so as to secure and harvest the fish, game, roots and berries which formed their food supply, and that they were, as yet, unfitted and untrained for the irksome confinements and labors of farm life and had neither the experience, means nor equipment to successfully maintain themselves as farmers, Chief Garry used his influence against the movement.[9]

Later in August, 1877, partially for the purpose of impressing on the Spokanes the threat of the Government to move onto a reservation *west* of the Columbia all Spokane Indians who refused to take up land in severalty, six companies of troops, under command of Colonel Wheaton, in conjunction with the Indian Commissioner and Lieutenant Wilkinson of General Howard's staff, were stationed in the Spokane country. This act resulted in dissatisfaction among the Spokanes, dividing the tribe into two parties. One, the larger, headed by Spokane Garry, strenuously opposed the movement to expatriate them; the other, headed by William Three Mountains, a former pupil of the Rev. Elkanah Walker at the Tschimokaine Mission and a rival for leadership, enthusiastically promoted the enterprise to locate a party of Indian homesteaders on land some six miles below Deep Creek Falls, now known as Indian Prairie.

The futility of the enterprise was shown by the results. Only five families moved out to start the undertaking, and though the colony once numbered fifty persons, the Indians gradually sold and traded their holdings to the whites (often for the most ridiculous and inadequate considerations) and either moved to the Lower Spokane Reservation or resumed their place among the remaining members of the Middle and Upper Spokanes.

The failure of the enterprise confirmed the soundness of Spokane Garry's judgment in opposing the movement to have the Spokanes take up land in severalty; a judgment concurred in by experienced army officers thoroughly familiar with the Indian situation.[10]

THE FINAL FATE OF THE SPOKANES

The refusal of the Commissioners to grant to the Spokanes any part of their lands for a reservation and their insistence that the Spokanes all move to the Coeur d'Alene Reservation finally led to the signing of a treaty by the Spokanes for the relinquishment of their land titles. This treaty is set out in appendix "B"; under it Garry and some of the older chiefs were each to receive an annuity of $100.00 a year.

The present Indian encampment at Indian Canyon is at sufferance of Mr. Gavin C. Mouat, owner of the property.[11] The once numerous and powerful tribe has been reduced to a mere handful, and it is now only a question of a little time when the band will be but a memory.

FOOTNOTES TO CHAPTER IV

1   Serial No. 1051, 36th Cong., 1st S.H.E. Doc. 65, p. 121.

2   Serial No. 1051, 36th Cong., 1st S.H.E. Doc. 65, p. 149.

3   Chittenden's *Life and Travels of Father DeSmet*, Vol. 2, p. 969. Serial No. 1051, 36th Cong., 1st S.H. Ex. Doc. 65, pp. 142-3.

4   Chittenden's *Life and Travels of Father DeSmet*, Vol. 2, pp. 766-767.

5   *Reminiscences of H.T. Cowley*, Library of Spokane Historical Society, p. 7.

6   *My Life and Experiences*, General O.O. Howard, p. 435.

7   Statement of H.T. Cowley. Durham's *History of Spokane County*, Vol. 2, p. 111.

8   Curtis' *North American Indian*, Vol. 7, pp. 55, 62.

9   Statement of Rev. H.T. Cowley, Library Spokane Historical Society.

10   Report on the condition of the Indian tribes, Wash. Govt. 1867. "I should remove the Indians to new reserves remote from settlers. I am satisfied the Indian cannot improve in the vicinity of white settlers. It is best that the Indians' lands be held in common, provided they are managed by judicial laws and regulations, and executed by honest and competent agents. *The Indian cannot long possess land in person, as no law or regulation can reach the swindling movements and sagacity of the white man.*" —Colonel John T. Sprague, Appendix, pp. 427-432.

11   As a commentary on Indian character, Mr. Moat [Mouat] states that in the past 35 years during which he had permitted the Indians to camp on this land, he has never locked a hen house or outbuilding when absent, and though Indians are constantly coming and going, he has never had a single article of property stolen from his place.

THE GORGE OF THE SPOKANE
"All this land was mine—and my people's." —Garry.
Photograph taken in the early 1880's from a point near the south end of the present Monroe Street Bridge, now in the heart of the City of Spokane.

CHAPTER V

GARRY TRIED TO BECOME A CITIZEN AND HOMESTEAD HIS FARM

ld Spokane Garry was not a fool. Thirty years' experience with the Indian Department had gradually convinced the Chief that the chances for a Spokane Indian to save a part of his inheritance in the way of a reservation were pretty slight. As a matter of personal precaution, Garry endeavored to establish and maintain a homestead right to the land used and held by him as his home.

For many years Garry and his family had resided on and cultivated a fine piece of farm land enclosed with a log fence, in what is now described as the west one-half of the northwest quarter of section 2, township 25 north, range 43, E.W.M., situated a short distance east of the present town of Hillyard, Washington. The treaty of 1887 was supposed to protect the Indian title to these homesteads.[1]

In the year 1888, while Garry and his family were at the temporary camp on the south side of the river during the fishing season, he heard that white men had taken possession of his farm. Together with his family, Chief Garry went at once to his land, and was told by the men in possession to keep off the place. Garry's farm was in crop at the time. Chief Garry endeavored in every peaceful way to recover possession from these trespassers, one of whom afterwards transferred his claim to the land to the late F. Lewis Clark, who secured title thereto from the Government. Immediately after seizing possession of Garry's land and filing thereon at the United States Land Office, this claimant procured a mortgage loan thereon for

$500.00; this indicated that the land was of some value.[2]

A short time before his death, Chief Garry procured a hearing on his claim to the land before United States Commissioner Skeels, in which testimony was adduced that he had long lived on the land and had endeavored to become a citizen of the country in order to become a legalized free holder, and that he held the land in question as a homestead with a squatter's right until the white men seized possession and drove him off. At the time the contest was heard Garry's homestead was reputed to be worth $25,000. Chief Garry died before decision was rendered against his claim. The government record in this case has been destroyed.[3]

The experience of Spokane Garry was typical of that of many of the Spokanes. Time and again white settlers went on the land cultivated and held by the Indians, dispossessing them, and frequently giving them a parting kick. Some fared a little better. Tim-mid-del-que and three other Indians driven off from their lands at Selheim Springs were given a second-hand saddle. Solomon Scott and Thomas Garry, driven from their land in the vicinity of Spokane Garry's farm, were given $13.00 by the man who dispossessed them; and old John Stevens, who fared better than most, was given the munificient sum of $30.00 by the magnanimous white man who drove him from his home.[4]

GARRY'S ATTITUDE TOWARD THE WHITE SETTLERS

The first instance of a white man (other than the fur traders and missionaries) settling in the Spokane country was that of old Solomon Pellitier (*sic*), who had settled on the old Walker-Eells mission site, with Garry's permission, prior to Governor Stevens' arrival in 1853.[5] The following year Messrs. Owen and Gibson, cattle men, maintained a considerable herd of horses and cattle in the Spokane Valley, with the consent of Spokane Garry, and the other chiefs. From these dates on Garry maintained a continued and consistent policy of friendly acquiescence in the settlement of the country by the whites, at the same time endeavoring to make a firm and determined stand against the continual encroachment of the settlers and the efforts of the Government to crowd the Indians from their favorite camping and fishing grounds, and to appropriate without compensation the fields and gardens which the Indians had maintained many years prior to the arrival of the first white settler.

"Garry kept telling the Spokane Indians to be peaceful while the white men were taking away the Indians' land. * * * * He asked the white people to leave the land of the Indians alone until the Indians could get paid for it, then, he told the white people, they could have the land from the Indians."[6]

GARRY AIDED IN THE CONSTRUCTION OF THE MULLAN ROAD

Spokane Garry aided in the building of the Mullan Road. During the winter of 1859-60, for the purpose of gathering statistics as to the snowfall and the practicability of building a road through that section of the mountains. Chief Garry carried the mail for Lieutenant Mullan from the Spokane Country to Fort Benton, Montana, by way of Clark's Fork.[7] In his report Lieutenant Mullan states that the Clark's Fork route was thus established to be more advantageous than the one over which the road was constructed. In addition to this, Spokane Garry, as shown by his letters on the subject, not only consented to rights-of-way through his country for railroad and wagon roads, but by his acts and conduct greatly assisted in procuring the assent of other Indian tribes to the construction of the roads and railroads.

GARRY'S FRIENDLINESS TOWARD THE WHITES

From his earliest youth to the time of his death Spokane Garry maintained a faithful friendship towards the whites. During his entire life, whenever any hostile acts against the whites were threatened by any of the neighboring tribes, or by any of the Spokane Indians, Garry was prompt to warn the whites of their danger. In 1848, after the Whitman massacre, when the Cayuse Indians were threatening to invade the Spokane country and to burn and destroy the Walker-Eells mission, Spokane Garry informed the missionaries that if the Cayuses crossed the Spokane River he would lead the Spokanes to meet and stop them. In 1856 Garry advised Governor Stevens as to the hostile attitude of some of the tribes, and as to the safest route by which he could reach Olympia. Mention has already been made of Garry's report of the Yakima murders to Indian Agent Bolon, and his advice to John Owen in 1858 as to the hostile attitude of the Coeur d'Alene Indians. During the Nez Perce war, and during every other Indian scare and excitement up to the time of his death, Spokane Garry continually exercised his influence to prevent any hostilities, and continually assured the white settlers, among whom he had many staunch friends, that he would give them timely warning in case of any danger from the Indians.[8]

CHIEF SPOKANE GARRY
Drawing courtesy of Jerome Peltier.

FOOTNOTES ON CHAPTER V

1   A copy of the treaty with the Spokanes made in March, 1887, is set out in the Appendix hereto. Note Article 4 thereof.

2   The records in the office of the County Auditor of Spokane County, Washington, show that on August 3, 1888, Receiver's receipt was issued by the U.S. Land Office to Schuyler D. Doak and recorded on August 30, 1888, in Book "X" of Deed Records of Spokane County, at page 285. That on August 30, 1888, on security of the land, Mr. Doak procured a loan of $500.00, the mortgage being recorded on August 30, 1888, in Book P of Mortgages, at page 240. The records show that on February 27, 1890, Mr. Doak conveyed the land to F. Lewis Clark by deed recorded in Book 17 of Deed Records, at page 496. U.S. patent to the land was not issued and recorded until April 23, 1892, after Garry's death, and is recorded in Book "I" of Deed Records, page 345.

3   *The Spokesman* (Spokane), January 14, 1892, p. 5. Letter Department of Interior, Library Spokane Historical Society.

4   *Pioneer Reminiscences of Milton S. Bentley.* Statement of Thomas Garry, *et al.*, *supra.*

5   Account of Governor I.I. Stevens. Pacific Railroad Reports.

6   Statement of Thomas Garry, *et al.*

7   Mullan's report on the construction of the military road, p. 19.

8   Journal of Mary Walker, 1848. Statement of H.T. Cowley.

MRS. CHRISTINE ELLENWOOD'S SON JIM AND HIS GRANDMOTHER, ANNIE NOSER. COURTESY OF RICHARD T. LEWIS.

SPOKANE GARRY
Head Chief of the Spokane Indians. Photograph taken about
1880.

CHAPTER VI

GARRY'S APPEARANCE

Spokane Garry, as known to those now living, was a small pot-bellied, shrivelled, blear-eyed old man, short in stature, dressed in citizen's clothing and wearing his hair cut short. Although over seventy years of age in the early '80's, he was still tough and wiry and able to endure great fatigue.[1]

Spokane Garry and his old white horse, shown in the accompanying illustration, were, in early days, familiar figures about the City of Spokane, which Garry, a dispossessed sovereign, saw rise about the Falls of Spokane, and attain, in his life time, a population of thirty-one thousand people; later Chief Garry's face was made familiar to another generation by an engraving on the checks of the Fidelity National Bank, a pioneer banking institution of the Spokane country.

Notwithstanding his lack of imposing stature, Spokane Garry in his prime carried himself with such an air of dignity and independence that it was apparent, even to a stranger, that he was a personage. Some of the early settlers and Government officials with whom Garry came in contact seem to have taken offense at and resented Garry's manner of equality. Spokane Garry bent to no man, and met on equal footing Governors, Generals, and Indian Commissioners.

Mr. James N. Glover mentions as an incident of General Howard's council held with the Spokane Indians in 1877, that after couriers had been sent out to call the Indians together, and they had gathered for the council, Spokane Garry rode in on horseback to the top of the bench above the council ground, which was held on the low ground at the extreme western edge of "Union Park"; tied his horse, and lay down to rest, refusing to comply with General Howard's impatient request that he join the council until he had fittingly refreshed himself, when he leisurely descended to the council ground.

When asserting the rights of the Spokanes to their lands, Spokane Garry was aggressive, both in speech and manner. In public he often wore a very firm, almost pugnacious expression; his chin, which seemed to be thrust out and emphasized by the firm closing of his lips, indicated a stubborn determination in keeping with his speech.

In his old age Spokane Garry appeared what he was: a poor, homeless, discredited old man, whose principal problem was to procure sufficient food and clothing to keep himself and his old blind wife alive. Thoughtless people made fun of him; hoodlums annoyed him and his family. In old age Garry's expression changed from aggressive firmness to patient submission. Through different causes: the disaffection of those of the tribe who had become Catholics; the rivalry of William Three Mountains; the success of Chief Whistle-Possum (Lot) in securing a reservation at the mouth of the Spokane River (the so-called Spokane Reservation); his own failure to secure any reservation for the Middle and Upper Spokanes; the aggressions of the white settlers; and the indifference displayed toward him by Government authorities, Indian agents, missionaries and many of the settlers, Spokane Garry's prestige with the Indians had been totally destroyed, and by the latter '80's his followers had been reduced to a mere handful.

GARRY'S DISPOSITION

Like most Indians, Spokane Garry was somewhat gruff and reticent when meeting white men for the first time, a characteristic which led some people, who never got acquainted with him, to conclude that he was of a rather sullen and morose disposition.

Spokane Garry went slowly with strangers. If he disliked a person, he left that person alone. It was only among friendly whites who had gained his confidence that he was talkative; to those he liked and trusted he would talk freely about Indian affairs and discuss his troubles and experiences. He possessed a dry wit, and was good-natured and intelligent in social intercourse with friends and sincere in his own beliefs and judgment, while maintaining a catholic tolerance for the opinion of others. Defeat, poverty and discredit did not, to outward appearances, embitter his spirit. To his last breath he expressed a firm confidence that the whites would eventually make proper compensation to him and his tribesmen for the land taken from them.[2] In his family relations Spokane Garry appears to have been kind, considerate and affectionate; several nephews, brought up by him in his family, speak of him still with noble regard.

GARRY'S MANNER OF LIVING

Prior to the loss of his farm in the latter '80's, Garry was a man of considerable wealth. He had a large herd of Indian horses, some cattle, and farm equipment, and raised considerable grain and vegetables, which were disposed of either in barter with the other Indians or with the early white settlers. His lodge was a model of neatness, and, as we have mentioned heretofore, was commented on by Mr. George Gibbs in 1853, as surpassing in neatness and comfort anything which the Stevens party had seen.[3]

Throughout his life Garry dressed in the costume of the whites, though preferring a blanket to an overcoat for wear in cold weather. His family also dressed in the costume of the whites, and in the early days lived in considerable comfort, keeping on hand supplies of tea, coffee, sugar and flour, commodities which some few of the first white settlers in the vicinity did not always possess.

GARRY'S LAST YEARS

Driven from his land, Spokane Garry was unable to afterwards secure another farm, and his circumstances rapidly changed for the worse. Of his large herd of horses, the greater part were stolen from him by the whites, principally by transient miners passing through the country in the early days, going to and from the various mining stampedes, and by professional horse thieves. His herd of cattle was killed off from time to time to supply meat for his family. In his latter years Spokane Garry was very hard up; the only money which the old chief obtained was an occasional ten or fifteen dollars, the price received from the sale of one of his horses. During the last years of his life, subsistence depended almost entirely upon the charity of chance, supplemented by the occasional earnings of his daughter, Nellie, a strong, honest, industrious woman, who did washing for the early settlers before the advent of the Chinaman and the steam laundry. The writer, when a boy, remembers taking an occasional ride on Nellie's pony while she was doing up the family washing.

After he was driven from his farm near Hillyard, Garry was forced to return to the tent life of his forefathers, and he established a camp, with a number of his relatives, on the second bench west of Hangman Creek, a little north of where the present concrete bridge crosses the Hangman Creek gorge at Seventh Avenue in the City of Spokane. There were six or eight tepees in this camp, but the Indians were subjected to so much annoyance by idle boys and hoodlums that they were unable to remain there, and Garry and his daughter, Nellie, finally procured the consent of Mr. Gavin C. Mouat for the removal of their camp to land owned by Mr. Mouat near Indian Canyon; and the Indian camp was moved to its present location on Mr. Mouat's property, where it has been maintained ever since by some of the homeless Spokane Indians.

At this time Garry's family consisted of his wife, Nina, who was blind, and his daughter, Nellie. Several of Garry's relatives lived at the camp; among them two nephews, Thomas Garry, now an elder of the church at Wellpinit, Washington, and Titus Garry, now an Indian policeman on the Spokane Indian Reservation, at Miles, Washington.

Spokane Garry seems to have taken good care of his old, blind wife. He would lift her on and off his horse, and for riding would carefully tie her on the saddle and then patiently and carefully lead the horse from place to place. From accounts of Mr. Mouat and others, it appears that he was always very kind and attentive to her.[4]

SPOKANE GARRY'S DEATH

Though he patiently waited nearly five years for our grateful and benign Government to pay him the paltry annuity of $100.00 a year which had been guaranteed him by the treaty of 1887, the old chief never received a cent of it.[5] Spokane Garry died in poverty and neglect at his camp at the Indian camping ground on Mr. Mouat's place, west of Hangman Creek, in Indian Canyon, on the 14th day of January, 1892, at 1 o'clock in the morning. He had been confined to his couch for more than eleven weeks; the cause of his death was old age, hastened by congestion of the lungs. When Garry was first taken sick, Mr. Mouat, an old friend, came into Spokane and consulted Mr. Harry Lane Wilson, now late Ambassador to Mexico, and the two engaged Dr. Harvey, a pioneer physician, to attend him. When Garry died, Billy Nolan (then bailiff for the Honorable R.B. Blake, and now holding a similar position under the judge's son, Judge Bruce Blake) went out with Mr. S.M. Smith, a pioneer undertaker, and prepared Garry's remains for burial.

Garry's funeral was conducted by the Rev. Dr. Mundy of the First Presbyterian Church of Spokane, on Saturday, January, 16, 1892, and his remains were buried at Greenwood Cemetary in the City of Spokane.

Garry's estate, which consisted of ten lean and flea-bitten cayuses, was administered by R.E. Porterfield, a rising young lawyer, now Secretary of the Citizens' Saving & Loan Society of the City of Spokane; Attorney W.D. Scott of Spokane, then just commencing the practice of law, represented Garry's daughter, Nellie. Of the ten cayuses constituting the estate, only two or three were ever located, the rest having been stolen; and the estate being insufficient to pay the expenses of his burial, the deficit was paid out of the pauper fund of Spokane County. Garry's grave for the last quarter of a century has been marked by a small wooden cross, on which may be read the legend, ''Indian Chief Gerry.''

WILLIAM S. LEWIS
FOOTNOTES FOR CHAPTER VI

1   Nearly all the Northwest Indians on attaining old age are afflicted with red and inflamed eyes, caused by the smoke of their lodge fires, blindness frequently results. For description of Garry see statement of H.T. Cowley; also General Howard's *Life and Experiences*, pp. 434-5; statement of John T. Davie and Gavin C. Mouat.

2   Statement of Nellie Garry.

3   See also statement of Gavin C. Mouat.

4   Statement of Gavin C. Mouat.

5   "After a pledge or promise of money it has always taken a long time to get the necessary appropriation through both Houses of Congress. No officer or agent can transfer his feelings of sympathy to our legislators. Often for years and years solemn pledges made to Indians—I state it with sorrow,—have remained unfulfilled." General O.O. Howard's *Life and Experiences*, p. 473.

Spokane Garry around 1861 at Fort Colvile.
Courtesy of David H. Chance and the Royal Engineers
Corps Library.

PART II

CASE AGAINST GARRY

GAMBLING

t is charged that Chief Garry gambled. He did. Spokane Garry seems to have possessed the usual Indian propensity for gambling, which was one of the few pastimes of the Indians wherein they could match their wits and acumen, one against the other. In reports of Wilkes' expedition in 1840, Spokane Garry is referred to indirectly by members of Lieutenant Johnson's party as an Indian chief who spoke English and who stated to them that at one time his authority was great over his tribe, but that owing to his propensity for gambling, he had lost all his influence.[1]

PLAYING CARDS

Governor George Simpson, previously mentioned, who passed through the Spokane country in 1841 on his celebrated journey around the world, saw his former protege in an Indian camp on the banks of the Pend d'Oreille River, near the site of the present town of Newport, Washington. Governor Simpson wrote that he found Spokane Garry sitting in a card game, played by the Indians with cards obtained from the American fur trappers in the Snake River country. He remarked on the apparent eagerness with which the naked and hungry savages thumbed and turned the black and greasy pasteboards, and stated that there could be but little doubt as to who was the master spirit in the game.[2] The Governor also, rather ill-naturedly, adds that Spokane Garry had relapsed into his original barbarism, taking as many wives as he could get, and becoming a gambler, losing all he had and all he could beg or borrow.[3] With commendable self-restraint, the honorable gentleman refrained from adding the words "or steal" to his commentary. There may have been some personal reason for this rather severe arraignment, as the Governor states that Garry refused to come out of the tent "to shake hands with an old friend" (Simpson).[4] His severe characterization of Spokane Garry was not concurred in, either by the early missionaries or the members of Governor Isaac I. Stevens' party, who visited Spokane House and were entertained by Garry at his lodge some twelve years later, and is disproven by the many known facts as to Garry's life.

There seems to have been a period in Garry's life, from 1837 to 1842, when, between 25 and 30 years of age, Garry abandoned his leadership of the Indians and his efforts for their improvement, and indulged in gambling, and relapsed back into savagery to some extent. This was contemporary with the arrival of the Protestant missionaries, and the writer has thought that Garry's conduct might have been caused by discouragement, pique and resentment on account of criticism made by the missionaries, and their ignoring him and his numerous efforts to enlighten and educate his tribe.

DRINKING

It is also charged against Spokane Garry that he drank intoxicating liquors. In common with most Indians, Spokane Garry had a liking for the "Boston man's fire water" and in his later years when he was a decrepit old man, Spokane Garry drank. It was only on very rare occasions, however, that Spokane Garry ever drank to excess or "got drunk." On one occasion, it is recalled by "old-timers" that Spokane Garry got drunk and was put into the town jail over night. Garry, however, took the matter in the right spirit, saying the next morning that it served him right, as he had no business to get drunk.[5]

GARRY'S GENERAL BAD REPUTATION IN HIS OLD AGE

Spokane Garry, during the last years of his life, was not given a good character by many of his contemporaries. The Rev. H.T. Cowley, a pioneer of 1874, says:

"Few, either Indians or white, among those I met from 1874 on spoke well of him." —Statement, Library Spokane Historical Society.

"He was a weak and vacillating character, crafty and unreliable." —Durham's History of Spokane County, Vol. I, p. 247.

J.M. Glover, "The Father of Spokane," has called Garry "an old skulker and hypocrite." —Durham's History of Spokane County, Vol. I, p. 351.

Major R.G. Gwydir has called him "kultus." —Statement, Library Spokane Historical Society.[6]

GARRY'S REPUTATION DISCUSSED

An investigation of these charges develops that the following stories, relative to Garry, were commonly circulated among the "old-timers":

Major Gwydir:

> It was gossip among the early settlers that Colonel Wright had hung Garry's father and brother whom Garry had sent into Colonel Wright's camp as hostages in his stead."
>
> My interpreter, Bob Flet, informed me that when Garry was captured and taken before Colonel Wright, who ordered his execution, frightened at the dread sentence, Garry hastened to state that he had a cousin and an uncle who were fighting warriors, and that if Colonel Wright would spare his life he would send for these two relatives, whom Colonel Wright might hang in his place. Colonel Wright agreed to this, and Garry sent word to his two kinsmen, who promptly gave themselves up, were tried, and hanged.

No father, brother, cousin or uncle of Spokane Garry, nor any Spokane Indians were hung by Colonel Wright: the reports of Col. Wright show that the Indians hung by him were all from tribes other than the Spokanes. Bob Flet was a Canadian-French Catholic, unfriendly to Garry. His stories were untrue, even though no malice may have prompted them.

Rev. H.T. Cowley states:

> William Three Mountains was not friendly to Garry, and he used to talk freely with me. He told me that Spokane Garry had taken part in the fights against the whites, and that when he saw that the Indians were conquered in the fight with Colonel Wright, he ran away and kept out of Colonel Wright's reach. William Three Mountains also told me that Colonel Wright had said that if he could get hold of Spokane Garry he would hang him.

The official records show that this account was also untrue. Spokane Garry, far from running from Colonel Wright, was frequently at the Colonel's camp, and at the Colonel's request assembled the Spokane and neighboring Indians for the council held at Smith's Ford in September, 1858. As one eye-witness states: "He (Garry) always had free access to the camp whenever he came to it."[7] William Three Mountains was unfriendly to Garry and on many occasions endeavored to undermine his authority and influence both with the Indians and the whites, and a rival who endeavored to supplant Spokane Garry as a leader of the Spokane Indians. His story, even though prompted by no malice or self-interest, was untrue in fact.

The Rev. H.T. Cowley relates another story concerning Spokane Garry:

> I met Mr. Tom Brown, an eighth Cree Indian, who had a fine farm at Chewelah, and was an old settler there and highly esteemed. Mr. Brown told me that before the fight with Colonel Wright, Spokane Garry had stopped at his place on his way to Colville, and had told him he was on his way to Colville to stir up the chiefs to resist Colonel Wright, and that he was promising them all the spoils in the event of the defeat of the Americans. This rumor in regard to Garry having participated in the hostilities was very persistent and was the cause of the prejudice which the early settlers had against Garry.

The only truth we can ascertain in the statement of Mr. Brown is that at the time of the battles of Four Lakes and Spokane Plains,

THE CASE OF SPOKANE GARRY

Spokane Garry did make a trip to Colville, and may have stopped at Brown's place on the way up. Spokane Garry's object and purpose in going to Colville was, as has been previously mentioned, to secure supplies to carry on his harvesting, in which he was then engaged; and, in view of Garry's consistent conduct, the repeated statements of himself and others that he took no part in the hostilities, and the record he made of his friendliness towards the whites, the finding must be against the truth of Mr. Brown's statement.

With reference to the statement of Mr. Glover that Garry was a "skulker and a hypocrite," no evidence has been found to substantiate their charges. Upon personal inquiry, Mr. Glover has said these terms were frequently applied to Garry by settlers who came in the '70's and the '80's, but that he has no personal knowledge of any wrong or questionable conduct by Spokane Garry justifying these terms as applied to the aged chief by the "old-timers."

Contrary to "skulking," Garry's conduct and speech were positive, even aggressive at times. From his speeches, letters and conversation, no person need, at any time, have had any doubt as to the position which Spokane Garry took upon any matter.

The same can be said as to the charge that he was a "hypocrite." Mr. Gavin C. Mouat, who perhaps knew Garry better than any other white man now living, says:

> He and I were good friends. He would come to my house lots of times and tell me his troubles. He was a sensible man in lots of ways and I have always thought that he was honest, sincere and truthful. Garry and his people were all Presbyterians, and Garry, himself, impressed me as being a sincere, religious man."

As to the charge that Garry was a "weak and vacillating character": If the charge of weakness was merely reference to Garry's frailties in the way of gambling and drinking, the charge of weakness may, to that extent, stand. Spokane Garry, if alive, would himself frankly confess to these failings. But Garry was neither weak nor vacillating in his purpose, and the record of his life shows fifty years of patient, persistent and determined effort on his part to keep peace with the whites and to preserve to himself and his tribe some portion of their heritage.

As to the charge that Garry was "crafty and unreliable": It will be admitted that, in the sense that he knew to some extent how to anticipate and combat the efforts of covetous white men and Government officials to extinguish the title of the Spokane Indians to their land, Spokane Garry was "crafty." General Howard stated that Garry "could filibuster like a Congressman." In any other sense the term can not be applied to him. Neither can he be called "unreliable." No person ever placed confidence in Spokane Garry and found him wanting.

It has also been charged that: "Spokane Garry gave the Indians bad advice and protected Indians who were charged with horse and cattle stealing." —Major Gwydir.

Among the white men, early settlers in the Spokane country, were a few well-known horse and cattle thieves, and a great deal of the early horse and cattle stealing committed by these white men was craftily charged by them to the Indians. An Indian may occasionally have stolen a horse in retalitation for the frequent thefts of Indian horses by the whites. Occasionally a hungry Indian may have slaughtered and eaten white men's cattle found on the range, and in doing so to sustain life, the Indians probably did not consider that they were more than playing even for the many losses they had suffered at the hands of the whites. If Spokane Garry did occasionally attempt to shield some such ignorant tribesman from the harsh consequences of the white man's laws, the writer would not regard such action by old Garry as particularly reprehensible under all the circumstances in the case. However, the writer has not been able to discover any facts to substantiate even this charge.

FOOTNOTES FOR PART II

1   U.S. (Wilkes) exploring expedition, Vol. 4, p. 459.

2   *Journey Around the World,* George Simpson, p. 144.

3   *Journey Around the World,* George Simpson, p. 145.

4   *Journey Around the World,* George Simpson, p. 145.

5   Statement of John T. Davie.

6   In Justice to these men it should be stated that these statements were made by them in good faith and in honest reliance on their truth, and that such reports were commonly circulated among and believed by a large part of the early settlers in the Spokane country.

7   John E. Smith, a pioneer of the Spokane country, Washington Historical Quarterly, Vol. 7, p. 270.

ELKANAH WALKER

SPOKANE GARRY'S GRAVE
Photograph by Palmer, Spokane, 1916. Spokane Indians, left
to right: Moses Phillips, Thomas Garry, William Three
Mountains, Alec Pierre and Charlie Warner.

PART II

CONCLUSION

The circulation of unfounded charges of this nature among "old-timers," who honestly believed that such reports were true, was the cause of the bad name given to Spokane Garry in his old age. But all pioneers were not deceived by these reports.

John T. Davie:

"The best citizens regarded old Spokane Garry as an Indian gentleman. Others among the rougher classes poked fun at him and disliked him."

W.D. Scott:

"Garry was a pretty nice old Indian."

For a quarter of a century old Spokane Garry has been in his grave, and, like Duncan, "After life's fitful fever he sleeps well." The faults and failings of the old chief, his gambling, his drinking, no longer peeve an arrogant generation, some of whom condescended to furnish him and his tribe with liquor, and others of whom were willing to gamble with them and win their money and property. Looking back, it appears rather strange that the early settlers, whose common club and social meeting place was the "saloon," and many of whom drank down their "three fingers" of straight rye at one gulp and scorned a "chaser," should condemn old Spokane Garry for drinking. The real reason for this condemnation was the prevailing sentiment that no Indian was any good, and that in their insistence on their claims to the land they were trespassers and a nuisance. Under such circumstances, any charge, however trivial or groundless, was sufficient excuse for the expression of the common contempt and dislike for the Indians.

Chief Garry's principal impediments, a fine farm and large band of Indian ponies, were not permitted to embarrass his old age. The superior whites relieved him of both.

The writer has no intention of casting any reflection on the pioneers as a whole, most of whom were representatives of the finest type of man and womanhood, which our country has produced: for the rest, candor compels us to state that there was also a fair assortment of rogues on the frontier in early days who had little respect for the rights or property of anyone, least of all the Indian; and it is a regretable fact that among the better class of settlers, who crowded them out, the Indians were generally regarded as outcasts, and it was their accepted maxim "That the only good Indian is a dead one." Even among the so-called better element, in early days, were "many greedy settlers who believed that Indians had no rights which a white man ought to respect."[1]

Spokane Garry died homeless and in poverty. A crude wigwam which had been his last shelter from the winter's snow and cold became his mortuary on death. Crowded from their lands, disease and poverty had decimated his tribe, and his title of chieftain was in melancholy contrast with his impoverishment of body and the departure of his temporary power. About the only thing that Spokane Garry possessed when he died was a childish faith that the white men would eventually do the square thing and compensate him and his people for the land they had taken.

Viewed from the standpoint of accomplishment, Spokane Garry's life was a failure. For forty years following the coming of General I.I. Stevens, the first Governor of Washington Territory, Garry's constant effort was to save part of the lands of the Spokane Indians for his people. In this he failed.

At no time was Spokane Garry the leader of as numerous and powerful tribes as old Chief Com-com-ly, or Chief Sealth of the Suquamish tribe; though his influence was felt over a larger area of territory than that of either of these chiefs. Garry was not a warrior like Kamiaken or Joseph. In fact, looking back over Garry's life and the history of his times, it would appear that Spokane Garry might better have served his purpose and accomplished more for his people had he donned the war paint, roused up his tribesmen and killed some white men. By such conduct an occasional Indian, unnoticed before, has achieved fame, become a pampered pet of the Indian Department and grown sleek and fat on annuities presented to him by a grateful government.[2]

Another course Garry might have profitably pursued would have been to practice a servile submission to the various Indian agents and Government officials, and to have co-operated with them in their efforts to extinguish the Indian land titles, regardless of the interest of the Indians. The course which Garry adopted led to failure, and he died a poor, friendless and discredited old man.

In regard to the place which Spokane Garry is entitled to occupy in the history of the Northwest, it will not be claimed for him that "He was the greatest friend of the whites on this side of the mountains," as an enthusiastic Western admirer of old Chief Sealth has claimed for him,[3] though few Indians appear to have so well deserved that title as Spokane Garry.

If the writer were to characterize Spokane Garry, it would be as one of the most manly, humane and likable Indian characters known to Northwest history. However, it has not been left to this generation to write Spokane Garry's epitaph; other willing hands wrote it long ago:

"He is what he claims to be and what few are among these tribes, a chief." —George Gibbs in the *Pacific Railroad Reports*, Volume 1, page 414.

"Garry is a man of judgment, forecast and strict probity and great reliability." —Governor I.I. Stevens, *Pacific Railroad Reports*, Volume 12, page 148.

"An Indian chief, a white man in education and views of life." —Governor I.I. Stevens, Serial No. 882, 34th Cong., 1st Session S. Ex. Documents 66, page. 43.

Ex. Documents 66, page. 43.

"Garry was a man whose friendship for the whites over half a century made the settlement and development of a large part of the Inland Empire a comparatively easy task." —*Review,* Spokane, January 14, 1892, page 6.

"There are those among the pale face invaders of the Northwest who are grateful for substantial aid given them in the early days by the aged chieftain." —*The Chronicle*, Spokane, January 14, 1892, page 4.

"Spokane Garry had, from the earliest occupation of the country by white people, been a peace man." —Victor's *Indian Wars of Oregon*, page 496.

"Neither the solicitations of the warlike chief of the Nez Perces nor the thought of the encroachment upon his rights could induce Spokane Garry to wage battle against the whites." —*The Spokesman,* Spokane, January 14, 1892, page 5.

"So far as Garry's influence was felt among his people it was on the side of progress." —H.H. Bancroft's *History of Oregon*, Volume 1, page 340.

The case of Spokane Garry is not unique; the history of our relations with the Indians is replete with similar cases.

It is my sincere hope that Spokane Garry and all true "children of the sun" that take the long trail to the Happy Hunting Grounds, will there find some unappropriated spot whereon to rear their lodge poles, as beautiful as the earthly paradise from which they were roughly crowded by the ruthless and unsympathetic whites.

THE END

FOOTNOTES FOR PART III

1   *My Life and Experiences,* General O.O. Howard.

2   See Major Gwydir in Edwards' *History of Spokane County*, p. 16.

3   Frank Carlson, *Chief Sealth*, Bulletin University of Washington, Series 3, No. 2, page 7.

First and second markers of Chief Spokane Garry's grave. Courtesy of Alfred Biggel.

NELLIE GARRY
Daughter of Spokane Garry. Photograph by Angvire,
Spokane, 1916.

APPENDIX A

Preliminary Articles of a Treaty of Peace and Friendship between the United States and the Spokane Nation of Indians.[1]

ARTICLE 1. Hostilities shall cease between the United States and the Spokane Nation of Indians from and after this date.

ARTICLE 2. The Chiefs and Headmen of the Spokane Indians, for and on behalf of the whole nation, promise to deliver up to the United States all property in their possession belonging either to the Government or to individual white persons.

ARTICLE 3 The Chiefs and Headmen of the Spokane Indians, for and on behalf of the whole nation, promise and agree to deliver to the officers in command of the United States troops the men who commenced the attack upon Lieutenant Colonel Steptoe, contrary to the orders of their chiefs, and further to deliver as aforesaid at least one chief and four men with their families as hostages for their future good conduct.

ARTICLE 4. The chiefs and headmen of the Spokane nation of Indians promise, for and in behalf of the whole tribe, that all white persons shall at all times and places pass through their country unmolested, and further, that no Indians hostile to the United States shall be allowed to pass through or remain in their country.

ARTICLE 5. The foregoing conditions being fully complied with by the Spokane Nation, the officer in command of the United States troops promises that no war shall be made upon the Spokanes, and further, that the men delivered us, whether as prisoners or hostages, shall in no wise be injured, and shall, within a period of one year, be restored to their Nation.

ARTICLE 6. It is agreed by both of the aforesaid parties that this treaty shall extend to and include the Nez Perce Nation of Indians.

Done at the Headquarters of the expedition against the Northern Indians at camp on the Ned-Whauld (or Lahtoo),

Washington Territory, this twenty-third of September, eighteen
hundred and fifty-eight.

G. WRIGHT
Colonel 9th Infantry Commanding United States Troops.

POHLATKIN,
SPOKAN GARRY
SKUL-HUL, his X mark,
MOIST-TURM, his X mark
SKI-KI-AH-MEN, his X mark,
SHE-LUH-KI-ITS-ZE, his X mark,
MOL-MOL-E-MUH, his X mark,
KI-AH-MENE, his X mark,
HOH-HOH-ME, his X mark,
HUSE-TESH-HEM-HIAH, his X mark,
NUL-SHIL-SHE-HIL-SOTE, his X mark,
CHE-LAH-HIM-SHO, his X mark,
HUIT-SUTE-TAH, his X mark,
KEH-KO, his X mark,
QUALT-TIL-TOSE-SUM (or Big Star), his X mark,
CHEY-YAL-KOTE, his X mark,
QUOI-QUOI-YOU, his X mark,
IN-SHO-ME-NAY, his X mark
ITS-CHE-MON-NEE (son of Pohlatkin), his X mark,
SCHIL-CHA-HUN, his X mark,
MEH-MAH-ICHT-SUCH, his X mark,
BE-NOIT, his X mark,
SO-YAR-OLE-KIM, his X mark,
SE-MAY-KOH-LEE, his X mark,
SIL-SO-TEE-CHEE, his X mark,
SEE-CHEE-NIE, his X mark,
KO-LIM-CHIN, his X mark,
HO-HO-MISH, his X mark,

SKI-IME, his X mark,

SE-RA-MIN-HOME, his X mark,

WE-YIL-SHO, his X mark,

CHE-NE-YAH, his X mark,

SHO-MOH-IT-KAN, his X mark,

PE-DALTZE, his X mark,

WITNESSES:

E.D. Keyes, Captain 3d Artillery; Wm. N. Orier, Brevet Major United States Army; J.F. Hammond, Assistant Surgeon, United States Army; R.W. Kirkham, Captain, Assistant Quartermaster; F.F. Dent, Captain 9th Infantry; Charles S. Winder, Captain 9th Infantry; James A. Hardie, Captain 3d Infantry; A.B. Fleming, First Lieutenant 9th Infantry; Jno, F. Randolph, Assistant Surgeon, United States Army; R.O. Tyler, First Lieutenant 3d Artillery; H.B. Lyon, Second Lieutenant 3d Artillery; Lawrence Kip, Second Lieutenant 3d, Artillery; J. Howard, Second Lieutenant 3d Artillery.

Col. Morrison and Nellie, daughter of Chief Spokane Garry and his wife Nina, a Umatilla. Courtesy of Richard t. Lewis.

Spokane Garry's four bibles, hymnal and pipe.

While Richard Lewis and I were visiting Mrs. Christine Ellenwood (in her home) and Mrs. Josie Parr, we asked many questions about the Garry family. Just before leaving, I asked Mrs. Parr—"Some day would it be possible to see Spokane Garry's bibles and take pictures of them." She answered, "You can see them right now" and reached behind the heating stove withdrawing a paper shopping bag from there. The bag contained the four bibles. Mrs. Parr astounded us by saying "Take them to Spokane with you and take some pictures of them but be sure to return them soon." Needless to say we did so. Report of conversation March 16, 1962. Jerome Peltier. Photo courtesy of Richard T. Lewis.

APPENDIX B

AGREEMENT WITH SPOKANE INDIANS[2]

Articles of agreement made and concluded at Spokane Falls, in the territory of Washington, the 18th day of March, eighteen hundred and eighty-seven, by and between John V. Wright, Jarred W. Daniel, and Henry W. Andrews, Commissioners duly appointed and authorized, on the part of the United States, and the undersigned, Chiefs, Head-men and other Indians of the Upper and Middle bands of Spokane Indians, they being authorized to act for said bands by them.

ARTICLE 1

The aforesaid bands of Spokane Indians hereby cede to the United States all right, title, and claim which they now have or ever had, to any and all lands lying outside of the Indian reservations in Washington and Idaho Territories, and they hereby agree to remove to and settle upon the Coeur d'Alene Reservation in the Territory of Idaho.

ARTICLE 2

It is further agreed by the parties hereto, that said Indians will be permitted to select their farms and homes on a tract of land to be laid off and surveyed and the boundaries marked in a plain and substantial manner under the direction of the Secretary of the Interior, on said Coeur d'Alene Reservation, provided that in laying out said tract of land, the lands taken and occupied by the Indians now on said Coeur d'Alene Reservation shall not be interferred with; and it is further agreed that said Spokane Indians will take lands in severalty under and according to an act of Congress entitled ''An act to provide for the allotments of land in severalty to Indians on the various reservations and to extend the protection of the laws of the United States and the Territories over the Indians, and for other purposes," which act was passed and approved during the second Session of the Forty-ninth Congress, and is known as the Allotment Act.

ARTICLE 3

It is further agreed that the homes and lands selected, as provided for in the foregoing article, are to be and remain the permanent homes of the Indians, parties hereto, and their children forever.

ARTICLE 4

It is further agreed that in case any Indian or Indians, parties hereto, have settled upon any of the unoccupied lands of the United States outside of said reservation, and have made improvements thereon with the intention of perfecting title to the same under the homestead, pre-emption or other laws of the United States, and residing on the same at the date of the signing of this agreement, he or they shall not be deprived of any right acquired by said settlement, improvement or occupancy by reason of signing this agreement or removal to said Coeur d'Alene Reservation, and said tract or tracts of land shall continue to be held by said parties, and the same patented to them by the United States.

ARTICLE 5

In consideration of the foregoing cessions and agreements the United States agrees to expend for the benefit of said Indians, parties hereto, the sum of ninety-five thousand dollars, as follows, to-wit: For the first year, thirty thousand dollars, for the second year, twenty thousand dollars, and for each succeeding year thereafter for eight (8) years, five thousand dollars, said money to be expended under the direction of the Secretary of the Interior in the removal of the said Indians to the Coeur d'Alene Reservation, in erecting suitable houses, in assisting them in breaking lands, in furnishing them with cattle, seeds, and agricultural implements, saw and grist mills, threshing machines, mowers, clothing, provisions; in taking care of the old, sick and infirm; in affording educational facilities, and in any other manner tending to their civilization and self-support: *Provided*, that in case any of the money herein provided for is not used or expended in any year for which the same is appropriated, said money shall be deposited in the Treasury of the United States to the credit of the Indians, parties hereto, to be used for their benefit under the direction of the Secretary of the Interior.

ARTICLE 6

It is further agreed that in addition to the foregoing provisions the United States shall employ and furnish a blacksmith to do necessary work and to instruct the Indians, parties hereto, in these trades.

ARTICLE 7

It is further agreed that in the employment of carpenters, blacksmiths, teamsters, farmers, or laborers, preference shall in all cases be given to Indians, parties hereto, who are qualified to perform the work or labor.

ARTICLE 8

In order to encourage said Indians in taking allotments of land, and in preparing the same for cultivation, it is agreed that when all of said Indians shall have selected and shall have broken five acres or more on each farm, the sum of $5,000 in money shall be given them out of the funds herein provided and distributed pro rata among them, provided that in the discretion of the Secretary of the Interior and the Commissioner of Indian Affairs, a pro rata payment out of said fund may be made to any ten families who shall have complied with the provisions of this article as to breaking land.

ARTICLE 9

In consideration of the ages of Chiefs Louis, Spokane Garry, Paul Schulhault, Antarchan, and Enoch, the United States agrees, in addition to the other benefits herein provided, to pay to each of them for ten years the sum of $100 per annum.

ARTICLE 10

In case any Indian or Indians, parties hereto, shall prefer and elect to remove either to the Colville or Jocko Reservations, instead of to the Coeur d'Alene Reservation, and shall give reasonable notice of the same, after the ratification of this agreement by Congress, he or they shall be permitted to do so, and shall receive a pro rata share of all the benefits provided for in this agreement.

ARTICLE 11

This agreement shall not be binding on either party until the same is ratified by Congress.

In testimony whereof, the said John V. Wright, Jarred W. Daniel, and Henry W. Andrews, on the part of the Unites States, and the Chiefs, Head-men and other Indians, on the part of the Indians, parties hereto, have hereunto set their hands and affixed their seals this 15th day of March, A.D. 1887.

JOHN V. WRIGHT (seal)

JARRED W. DANIELS (seal)

HENRY W. ANDREWS (seal)

Signed with an X mark and seal:

Elijah; Curley Jim; Eneas; Sa-wap-a-louse; Frazy; Chief Joseph Skulhault; Chief Paul; Sale Spiley; Whisto So Jim; Paul Thomas; Charlie Louis; Buckskin Jim; Packing-his-hair; Qenant la com i con; John La Mar; Qiay quis to; Chief "Aantarcham"; Chief "Spokane Garry"; William Jackson; Quili Tah; Broken Tooth; John Stevens; Old Solomon; Sco Cow; Nuishels Smeya; Obed Jacobs; Thomas S. Garry; Solomon Scott; Joseph J. Wilson; Paul A. Garry; Levi; Chimmilichan; Shikinez; George; Ziomka; Joshua; Isaac; John Wilson; "See Mok Mosquetquat"; "The Mountain Turkey"; Billy; Lot; Elias; Stephen; Chilkenishin; Schietish; Chief Enock; Spokane George; Skulskullah; Shilchitemtoo; Chief Louis Welsholeg; Kampan Charley; Whitsotah; Peiresish; Kylminah; Louis; Philip; Antoine; Old Philip; Peter; Elick; Chetleskaimik (Three Books); Stwoichin; Kulzkoo; John; Silimihan; Skamtaikn; Light of the Belly;

Antoine; Quennemosco; Old John; Sakkon; Pascal, Tanuayakn; Zillon; (Augustus) Castah; Chestolo; Selotachan; Che-Squei-tah; Peter; Saltochasalchie; Eliquinch; Oltzschomak (Luke); Shiouitchan.

WITNESS:

    FRED R. MARVINS,

    SIDNEY D. WATERS.

    I, Robert Flett, United States Interpreter for the Colville Indian Agency, W.T., do hereby certify on honor that the foregoing agreement was carefully read in open council, and by me correctly interpreted, and that the contents thereof were fully explained to and fully understood by said Indians before the signing and sealing of the same.

his

ROBERT (X) FLETT.

mark

Dated Spokane Falls, W.T., March 18, 1887.

    SIDNEY D. WATERS.

    The Undersigned, members of the within named Spokane tribe of Indians, not being present at the signing and concluding of this agreement at Spokane Falls, W.T., having had the same fully interpreted to us, do this 27th day of April, 1887, fully agree to its provisions, and affix our names and seals at St. Ignatius Mission in the territory of Montana.

Signed with an X mark and seal:

    Baptiste Peon, Pierre, Michael, Joseph, David, Edmund, Wm. King, Francois.

WITNESS:

    THOMAS E. ADAMS.

I, Michael Revais, United States Interpreter for the Flathead Agency, Montana, do hereby certify on honor that the foregoing agreement was carefully read in open council, and by me correctly interpreted, and that the contents thereof were fully explained to and fully understood by said Indians before signing and sealing.

his

MICHAEL (X) REVAIS.

mark.

Dated Flathead Agency, Mont., April 28, 1887.

WITNESS:

THOMAS E. ADAMS.

HENRY A. LAMBERT.

CUSHING EELLS, D.D.
FOUNDER OF WHITMAN COLLEGE

FOOTNOTES ON THE APPENDIX

1   Manring's *Conquest of the Coeur d'Alenes,* p. 229. Also H. Ex. Doc. No. 2, pp. 407-8, 35th Congress, 2nd Session.

2   Ratified by Indian appropriation act of July 13, 1892 (See Vol. 27, p. 139, U.S. Stat.) six months after Garry's death.

JOSEPH GARRY ON FAR RIGHT AND UNKNOWNS. COURTESY OF JEROME PELTIER.

ETSHIIT

THLU

SITSKAI

THLU

SIAIS

THLU

Sitskaisitlinish.

LAPWAI

1842.

The title page from the book Etshiit, first book set in the Spokane language. Courtesy of Jerome Peltier.

BIBLIOGRAPHY FOR INTRODUCTION

Barker, Burt Brown (editor). *Letters of Dr. John McLoughlin Written at Fort Vancouver 1829-1832.* Published by Binfords and Mort for the Oregon Historical Society, Portland, Oregon, U.S.A., 1948.

Drury, Clifford Marrill. *First White Women Over the Rockies.* 3 vols., the Arthur H. Clark Co., Glendale, California, 1963.

_____. *Marcus and Narcissa Whitman and the Opening of Old Oregon.* 2 vols., the Arthur H. Clark Co., Glendale, California, 1973.

_____. *Chief Lawyer of the Nez Perce Indians 1796-1876.* The Arthur H. Clark Co., Glendale, California, 1979.

_____. *Nine Years With the Spokane Indians: The Diary 1838-1848, of Elkanah Walker.* The Arthur H. Clark Co., Glendale, California, 1976.

_____. *The Diaries and Letters of Henry H. Spalding and Asa Bowen Smith Relating to the Nez Perce Mission, 1838-1842.* The Arthur H. Clark Co., Glendale, California, 1958.

Dunbar, Seymour and Paul Phillips, editors. *Journals and Letters of Major John Own, Pioneer of the Northwest 1850-1871.* 2 vols., Edward Eberstadt, New York, 1927.

Heitman, Francis B. *HIstorical Register and Dictionary of the United States Army.* 2 vols., Washington, Government Printing Office, 1903.

Highberg, Kathryn Treffry. *Orchard Prairie, The First Hundred Years 1879-1979.* Ye Galleon Press, Fairfield, Washington, 1978.

Jessett, Thomas E. *Chief Spokan Garry 1811-1892, Christian, Statesman and Friend of the White Man.* T.S. Denicon & Co., Inc., Minneapolis, Minn., 1960.

Johnson, Donald R. (editor). *William H. Gray, Journal of his Journey East, 1836-1837.* Ye Galleon Press, Fairfield, Washington, 1980.

Merk, Frederick (editor). *Fur Trade and Empire. —George Simpson's Journal (1824-1825).* Cambridge, Harvard University Press and London, Humphrey Milford, Oxford University Press, 1931.

Peltier, Jerome. *A Brief History of the Coeur d'Alene Indians 1806-1909.* Ye Galleon Press, Fairfield, Washington, 1982.

_____. *Antoine Plante, Mountain Man, Rancher, Miner, Guide, Hostler and Ferryman.* Ye Galleon Press, Fairfield, Washington, 1983.

_____. *Warbonnets and Epaulets.* Payette Radio Ltd., 730 St. Jacques, Montreal 101, Canada.

NEWSPAPERS

Becher, E.T. *Sunday Spokesman-Review.* Inland Empire Sections, May 24, 1953, May 31, 1953 and June 7, 1953.

GOVERNMENT REPORTS

Message of the Governor of Washington Territory. Olympia, Edward Furste, Public Printer, 1857.

Report of the Commissioner of Indian Affairs. Government Printing Office, Washington, D.C., 1857.

Report of the Secretary of War. Washington, George W. Bowman, Printer, 1860, pages 301 to 306.

Reports of Exploration and Surveys to Ascertain the Most Practicable and Economical Route for a Railroad from the Mississippi River to the Pacific Ocean. Thomas H. Ford, Printer, Washington, 1860, Volume 12, part 1. Hereafter to be cited as R.R. Reports.

HISTORICAL QUARTERLIES

Pacific Northwest Quarterly. July 1940 and October 1940.

Washington Historical Quarterly. October 1916 and April 1917.

INTERVIEWS

Interview with Christine Ellenwood on July 10, 1958.

Interview with both Josie Parr and Christine Ellenwood on March 16, 1962.

Interview with Ignace Hayden Garry on October 12, 1961.

Taped interview with Ignace Hayden Garry with the date not known exactly.

Mrs. J.J. Brown's account is likely one that was made when William S. Lewis was interviewing pioneers for the Spokane Historical Society. He was Secretary of the Society at the time.

BIBLIOGRAPHY FOR TEXT
(Authorities cited only.)

Bancroft, H.H. *History of Oregon.* San Francisco, History Co., 1886.
_____. *History of the Pacific Northwest.* San Francisco, History Co., 1886.
_____. *History of Washington, Idaho and Montana.* San Francisco, History Co., 1890.

Carlson, Frank. *Chief Sealth.* University of Washington Bulletin, Series III, No. 2.

Chittenden, H.M. and A.T. Richardson. *Life and Travels of Father DeSmet.* F.P. Harper, New York, 1905.

The Chronicle, Spokane, Washington, January, 1892.

Congressional Documents, Serial Nos. 882, 889, 899, 972, 984, 1051, Washington Government.

Congressional Reports on Condition of the Indian Tribes. 1867, Washington Government.

Cox, Ross. *Columbia River.* 3rd. Ed., Colburn, London, 1832.

Curtis, Edward S. *North American Indian.* Volume 7, author, 1911.

Douglas, David. *David Douglas Journal.* Wesley & Sons, London, 1914.

Durham, N.W. *History of Spokane County.* S.J. Clarke Publishing Co., Spokane-Chicago-Philadelphia, 1912.

Edwards, Rev. Jonathan. *History of Spokane County.* W.H. Lever, 1900.

Eells, Myron. *Father Eells* Congregational Pub. Co., Boston, 1894.

Gannett, Henry. *Origin of Certain Place Names in the United States.* Government Printing Office, Washington, 1905.

Gibb, George. *Report 1, Pacific Railroad Report.* Washington Government, 1855.

Gonzaga Silver Jubilee Memoir. Gonzaga College, Spokane, 1892.

Gray, W.H. *History of Oregon.* Harris, Portland, Oregon, 1870.
_____. *W.H. Gray's Journal.* Whitman College Quarterly, Walla Walla, Washington, Vol. 16, No. 2, June, 1913.

Handbook of American Indians American Bureau of Ethnology, Washington Government, 1907.

House Es. Doc. No. 2, 25th Congress, 2nd Session.

Howard, Gen. O.O. *My Life and Experiences Among Our Hostile Indians.* Worthington, Hartford, 1907.

Kip, Lieutenant Laurence. *Army Life on the Pacific.* Redfield, New York, 1859.

Manring, B.F. *Conquest of the Coeur d'Alenes, etc.* John W. Graham & Co., Spokane, 1912.

Missionary Herald of 1840. Boston, Mass.

Mullan, John. *Report on Construction of Military Road.* Washington Government, 1863.

Olympia Standard. Olympia, Washington, February 15, 1879.

Pacific Railroad Reports. Volumes 1 and 12, Washington Government, 1855-1860.

Parker, Rev. S. *Journal of Exploring Tour.* Author, Ithaca, N.Y., 1838.

The Review. Spokane, Washington, January, 1892.

Ross, Alexander. *Fur Traders.* Smith, London, 1849.

Simpson, Governor George. *Journey Around the World.* Colburn, London, 1847.

The Spokesman. Spokane, Washington, January, 1892.

Stevens, Hazard. *Life of General I.I. Stevens.* Houghton, Boston, 1900.

Symons, Lieut. T.W. *The Upper Columbia River.* Wa. Library Spokane Historical Society.

Pioneer Reminiscences, Milton S. Bentley, Library Spokane Historical Society.

Pioneer Reminiscences, Rev. H.T. Cowley. Library Spokane Historical Society.

Pioneer Reminiscences, John T. Davie. Library Spokane Historical Society.

Pioneer Reminiscences, Major Gwydir, Library Spokane Historical Society.

Pioneer Reminiscences, Gavin C. Mouat. Library Spokane Historical Society.

Pioneer Reminiscences, W.P. Winans. Library Spokane Historical Society.

Statement of Curley Jim. Library Spokane Historical Society.

Statement of Nellie Garry. Library Spokane Historical Society.

Statement of Susan Michel. Library Spokane Historical Society.

Statement of Moses Phillips, Thomas Garry, Library Spokane Historical Society.

Index

Body Moved to New Site

The remains of Mrs. Spokane (Nina) Garry, widow of a chief of the Spokane Indian tribe yesterday were removed from her burial place at Fairfield and reinterred in the grave of her husband at Greenwood cemetery in Spokane.

Mrs. H. C. Faubion, a member of the Spokane Garry chapter of the Daughters of the American Revolution, said two great-granddaughters of Chief and Mrs. Garry attended the ceremony. They are Josie Parr and Christine Ellenwood, both of Worley, Idaho.

Chief Garry was a head of the Spokanes for 60 years prior to his death in 1892 in Indian Canyon. He was not permitted burial inside the cemetery until the early 1900s when the D. A. R. had his body removed from a place adjacent to the cemetery to the present grave, which is marked by an impressive monument the D. A. R. provided.

Smith's was in charge of the reburial yesterday. Members of the Garry chapter conducted the ceremony.

Article from the *Spokane Chronicle* of June 26, 1962 about the reinternment of Nina Garry, wife of Spokane Garry.

133

Left to right: Mrs. Christine Ellenwood, Mrs. Josie Parr, Ignace Garry, Reverend, Joseph R. Garry, Mrs. H.C. Faubion and unknown at the reinterment of Nina Garry in July of 1962. Courtesy of Richard T. Lewis.

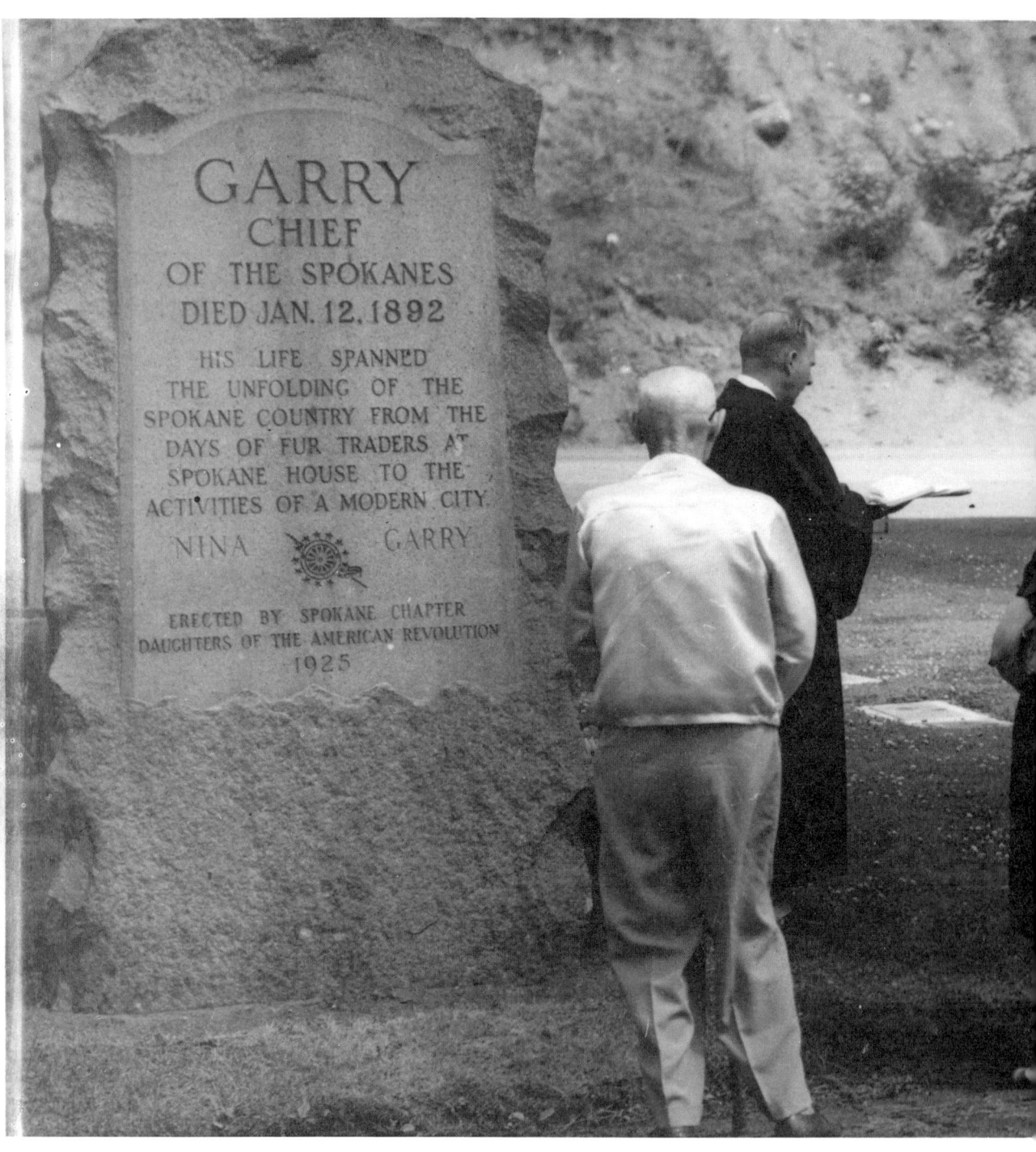

Left to right: Reverend, Mr. Brock with back to camera, Mrs. Josie Parr, Mrs. Faubion, Mrs. Christine Ellenwood (with shawl), Mrs. Brock with back to camera, Ignace Garry behind Joe Garry, Mable Frederick, ?, Edith Smith, and Jerome Peltier. Courtesy of Richard T. Lewis.

137

CHIEF SPOKANE GARRY

138

COLOPHON

The *William S. Lewis* book THE CASE OF SPOKANE GARRY *was printed in the workshop of Glen Adams, which is located in the sleepy farming village of Fairfield, southern Spokane County and Washington state. The text was set in fourteen point Garamond with the running head and page numbers in Feinen by Sharyn Brown using an Editwriter 7300 computer photosetter. Indexing of the book was by Sharyn Brown. The film was stripped by Sylvia Fenich. Photography-darkroom work was by Sylvia Fenich. The sheets were printed by Mike Fenich using a model KORS Heidelberg press. The sheets were folded by Garry Adams using a 22 x 28 Baum three stage folding machine. Assembly was by the Ye Galleon crew. The paper stock is seventy pound Island Offset, a Canadian sheet. Hard case copies were bound by Willem Bosch of Oakesdale, Washington assisted by his son, Gerrit Bosch, and Bill Harnois. The signatures were sewn by Juanita Hurlbert. Gold foil stamping of the cases was by Willem Bosch, Jr. Paper covered copies were bound by Glen Adams and Garry Adams. This was a fun project. We had no special difficulty with the work.*

Left to right: Ignace Gar
Ellenwood and Joseph
Garry at Greenwood Cem